Choose You First

One Woman's Journey Through Pain, Resilience and Hard-Won Healing.

A Powerful Reminder That Your Story Is Far from Over

Michelle Bishop

Copyright © 2024 by Michelle Bishop
All rights reserved.

No part of this book may be reproduced, distributed, or transmitted in any form or by any means, including photocopying, recording, or other electronic or mechanical methods, without the prior written permission of the publisher, except in the case of brief quotations embodied in critical reviews and certain other non-commercial uses permitted by copyright law.

Disclaimer

This book is intended for informational and educational purposes only. The author and publisher are not liable for any errors or omissions or for any outcomes related to the use of this information. Readers are encouraged to consult with professional advisors for specific advice.

ISBN (Paperback): 979-8-9917123-0-9

ISBN (Hardback): 979-8-9917123-2-3

ISBN (eBook): 979-8-9917123-1-6

First Edition: 2024
Acknowledgments of Trademarks

All product names, logos, and brands mentioned in this book are the property of their respective trademark holders. Mention of these names, logos, or brands does not imply endorsement.

To my forever inspiring grandma, my two incredible daughters, my beloved Richard, and my greatest love, Daddy.

This is just the beginning.

To receive updates from me, schedule a "Listening Session" and join the *Live Your Best YOU* Community, visit:

https://bishoplife.com/

Table of Contents

Welcome to Choose You First 1

Part 1: Life Is The Story 2

    Imprint 7
    Transition 47
    Life Shifting and Altering 63
    Falling For My Personal Beliefs 117
    New Explorations 135
    Chaos and Passion 167
    Discovering Who I Really Am 181

Part 2: Life Is The Lesson 205

    The Silent Warrior 207
    You Did Nothing Wrong 223
    Choose You First 237
    One More Thing 281

About the Author 287

Thank You 289

Welcome to Choose You First

I love that you and I are going to spend some time together. The book you have in your hands isn't just a book to help you step further, deeper, and bigger into your life, nor is it just one person's story. It's a little bit of both. Its purpose isn't to shock or lecture; it's to share—no more, no less.

Throughout my life, I've experienced immense pain, fear, loss, and isolation. I've also experienced tremendous love, companionship, joy, and growth. Through all those roundabouts, I've learned who I am and what I'm capable of, and above all, I've learned to love. Not just others but myself.

To help share what I've learned, I've broken this book into two parts. The first part is my story. Not every single tiny detail, but the broad strokes. Enough, I hope, to give you an insight into how a broken childhood can be healed and how, no matter how long it takes, you can find your true purpose.

I've called this book *Choose You First* because, as a woman, you probably don't. We're raised to put everyone ahead of us, and while that seems honorable, it often defeats our purpose. When we are broken down, we can't build anyone else up. When we are in great pain, it's hard to heal anyone. When we are exhausted, it's hard to raise others up.

We all come with baggage, history, complications, and messiness. I hope this book shows you that no matter how difficult things are, we're always stronger than we imagine. We always find a way. There's always love to be found. And it can always be found within.

I hope you enjoy the story, and I hope it helps you on your journey through your remarkable life.

With great love.
Michelle.

Part 1:
Life Is The Story

Imprint

Something happened when I was ten years old that changed me. It changed how I perceived and experienced my childhood, and it impacted every part of my life going forward. It happened in less than a minute. But that minute meant everything.

To understand why it had such an impact, we're going to start at the beginning. But before we do that, I want you to settle back and get comfortable because by the end of this book, you and I will have explored the impact childhood events can have on you and why nothing that happened when you were a child is your fault. Ever. That's just a fact.

So, from the beginning...

I was born in the 60s, a time when the rules of society were changing, as they do with every decade. My father was born in Pensacola, Florida, in the Panhandle, a place with deep Southern roots. My mother was from New York, a completely different world. The differences in their upbringings were immense.

They met in Gulfport, right outside of St. Petersburg, Florida (where I was born), at a little beach bar where all the law students went. It was a regular hangout at the time and is likely still there today.

My mom was working as a secretary for an attorney at the time, and it was common for girls like her to meet young attorneys in places like that.

My parents dated a little, attracted to each other physically at first, but their relationship really developed when my father needed a date for the various law school events.

Things moved quickly, and when my mother fell pregnant with me, my father was in his senior year of law school. Back then, if you got pregnant, you got married or the man bolted. That's how it was. My father hadn't even graduated yet or taken the bar exam. He shares the story of walking to the payphone to call his parents about the situation. His mother was very comforting and then deferred to his father. He was a military man and had spoken few words through my father's upbringing. Encouragement wasn't his go-to dialogue. He simply said, "Son, you need to marry her." That was the beginning.

I've always said how grateful I am that my dad chose to keep me in his life. It would have been easy for him to abandon the situation, but he didn't, and through the years, he did the best he knew how in a very difficult situation.

It was tough at the start. They struggled to make ends meet, and on top of that, they didn't really know each other. They were a young couple working things out as they went.

It didn't help that my mother came to the marriage with quite a lot of emotional and psychological baggage. Her early life had been difficult. Her mother had died when she was just fourteen, and she'd been physically abused by her father, who had uprooted her from New York and moved her to St. Petersburg, Florida when she was still a teenager.

My dad, on the other hand, came from a pretty stable background. His mother was a home economics teacher, and his father was a fighter pilot in the Navy. There was discipline, stability, and a lot of love and guidance from his mother, primarily because his father had been called to war and was essentially away for the first five years of his life. All that said, my dad was the second of four boys in his family, and he was raised without the level of mental chaos that had impacted my mother's early years so heavily.

So, with that as a backdrop, I was born to a couple who were attracted to each other but didn't know each other. My mother was handling mental stress my father didn't know about, and my father was trying to establish his career.

He worked six days a week in what was definitely not a nine-to-five job. As an ambitious young lawyer, he did whatever it took to climb the ranks so he could support his family. But with all his attention at work, he had no idea that chaos was taking root at home.

Looking back, my father didn't know the extent of my mother's struggles. She had a talent for creating a facade, revealing only what she wanted people to see. My dad included. What she didn't hide was the fact that she drank and smoked during all her pregnancies. In fact, for as long as I can remember, she had a drinking problem.

I'm not going to delve into every detail of those early, early years because, honestly, a lot of the memories are shrouded by a fog designed to protect young minds. A lot of what I do remember is made up of fragments, except for a few events that seared themselves into my young brain. As a result, as I share the early years with you, it'll feel like we're leap-frogging between memories. And you'll be right.

The best way I can think to describe how my memories are stored is to see my brain like a library. The walls from floor to ceiling are full of books. Each book is a memory. Every book contains wisdom and knowledge, experience and moments, some big and some small, that have happened through the years. Some of these books have never been taken off the shelf. They're dusty and they're forgotten, and that's where they belong. That's how we survive tragedy.

So, with that in mind, I'll jump ahead to the years my sisters were born.

A Young and Challenged Family

By the time I was six years old, my middle sister was four, and my youngest sister was a baby.

My dad was working all hours, and my mom wasn't coping with life, let alone parenthood. During those times the traditional role of the father was to provide for his family, and the mother took care of the house, cooking, cleaning and caring for the children. She lacked in almost every way for this role. Her upbringing and her mentality simply left her unable to cope with just about every aspect of running a home and raising children. As kids, we didn't know that her behavior wasn't normal because it was really all we had been exposed to in our lives. It was what it was.

In those very early years, I shared a tiny room in a tiny house with my younger sister Merina, 21 months my junior. I remember clearly reaching through the crib bars to calm her when she cried. If she continued to cry, it would only anger my mother and cause her to act out against my baby sister, physically shaking her and tossing her back in the crib, or going after me at three or four years of age. All of it frightening; none of it good. That's one of the few clear memories I have from those early years. Maybe that's a good thing because one of the other memories that I've never been able to clear from my mind is an event that occurred when I was around four years old.

Merina was sitting between my mom and me in the front seat of the car. It was the sixties. There were no seatbelt laws. It was a long and dusty road, with not much to see on either side. Suddenly, my mother opened the passenger door and tried to push us out. There was no warning. No words. She just opened the door and shoved.

I clung to the door handle, looking down at the gravel rushing beneath us. A man driving behind us honked his horn, trying to get her attention.

Eventually, she pulled over into a parking lot. The man came up to the car and said, "Your door's open!"

"Oh my gosh!" my mother replied, putting on a dramatic *how-did-that-happen* act. "I didn't realize!"

When the man left, her mood shifted. She turned on us. "Get on the floor and don't move!"

she screamed. My sister cried. I cried. She yelled for us to shut up. And she drove on.

Her anger was palpable and impossible to comprehend. And this wasn't unusual. We never knew when she would erupt or what form it would take.

One moment, she'd ignore us, and the next, she would put us in the bath, sometimes in water so scalding hot that it blistered our skin and other times so cold we froze. At night we'd go to sleep not knowing what we'd wake up to.

I have no idea, to this day, what demons drove her. In hindsight, I do know that she suffered from undiagnosed mental illness. It's the only explanation.

At the time, as happens in most cases of abuse, her actions never made me love her any less. They just left me more confused.

Dad Did What He Could

Time passed, we survived, my dad worked, and my mother's tirades got worse.

No matter what we did or didn't do, something always triggered her. When her anger reached a point we couldn't take, my sister would scream for my dad. "I want my daddy! I want my daddy!" Over and over. As you can imagine, this infuriated my mother, and she'd come after us.

I knew all my mother needed was to get hold of one of us. As soon as she did that, there would be violence, then it would be over for a moment. So, I'd shove my sister into a small cubby hole in the house, just a bench between two walls really, and I'd lay in front of her, shielding her from my mother. The trick was to lay far enough back so it wasn't easy for her to grab me. I was the oldest, so I endured the physical abuse. When it was over, my mother would calm down. And there'd be quiet for a moment.

The physical abuse was one thing. I got used to that. What I found more confusing and difficult to handle was the verbal abuse. Not just toward me, but toward everyone, especially the weakest and most vulnerable.

My mother would tell me over and over I was bad, that I wasn't a good girl. There was nothing, and I mean nothing that was right by her. It wasn't just me who endured this verbal assault, as soon as the doors closed, all of us got it.

I remember one particular moment when she called me a whore. I was probably six years old. I didn't know what the word meant, so I asked my father, "Daddy, what's a whore?"

"Why would you ask me that?" he responded, a little taken aback.

"Mommy says I'm a whore," I replied.

He brushed it off. "No, no, don't worry honey. She must have gotten confused. She didn't mean anything by that."

But how do you explain something like that to a child? You can't. It wasn't so much the word that hurt and confused me. I didn't know what it meant. It was the angry, jagged tone she used.

My father knew what was happening, I'm sure he tried to talk to my mother, but he didn't intervene within the earshot of small children.

He kept on working all hours, day and night, keeping up with the demands of the expectations that he had for himself, his family and society. While he did that, we did what we could to make it through each day, despite frequently being sent to bed at 4 p.m., without dinner. We could hear the other kids outside, playing around and enjoying their evening while we were stuck in our rooms.

When my father came home at night, he'd come to our room and ask, "Well girls, what did you do today?" We would be so excited to see him, soaking up all his safety and paternal love. Then he would ask, "So, what did you have for dinner tonight?" When we told him we hadn't had anything, he'd bring us food without my mother knowing.

It was better that way because if my mother found out what he was doing for us girls, she'd have unleashed a new level of fury on us. Unfortunately, those nights without dinner were common.

It probably didn't help that my mother had a compulsive relationship with food. We had more meat than most families since her father had been a butcher, and back then, beef wasn't something everyone could afford. Still, she'd force me to clear my plate, even though I was just a little kid and couldn't eat much. I tried all the tricks, like hiding food under the table or feeding it to the dog, but nothing got past her.

Anyway... I digress.

And Then There Were Three

By the time my youngest sister was born—she was five and a half years younger than me—things had changed. My dad had started his own practice and there was money coming into the family home. We had moved into a bigger house and our social scene elevated. My mother became more involved in the Country Club, and when my youngest sister was born, she had a private room, the perfect nursery, and was treated like the princess of the family.

It's like the idea of what life should be was coming true for my mother, and she was determined to maintain the image. Her determination showed up in a frenzy. Every time she threw a dinner party she would scream and shout to get us to clean the house until it was pristine. Then we'd have to be dressed just right to make sure the image of the perfect family was upheld. "Children are to be seen, not heard," was her cardinal rule.

These family and social gatherings were always chaotic, but not in the same way. The more the adults drank, the louder they became. To this day, I have always remained sensitive to loud noises.

Things were different with my father's family. They lived in Pensacola but would visit occasionally. It was always a joy for us to be able to visit them in the Panhandle of Florida. The 10-hour drive was never much fun, but my mother would give us cough syrup so we would sleep most of the drive. Funny, because to this day I become sleepy while driving distances in the car.

With no love from my mother, I found love anywhere I could. In particular, I absolutely soaked up the love that I received from my grandmother on my father's side while visiting her and the homestead there. It was filled with aunts and uncles, cousins, my grandparents. My grandma was the epitome of Southern grace: charming, smart, kind and filled with love. From the moment I was in her arms as a young baby till the day she died, I owe so much of my being to her. I also loved going to my Aunt Judy's house on my mother's side. She wasn't exactly maternal, but she was kind, and I knew what to expect when I was there. I wasn't going to be yelled at or punished for no reason, and that predictability was comforting.

A Childhood of Extremes

The first seven years of my life were lived in extremes, from violent instability to moments of excess.

Christmases were beyond extravagant, with so many presents I can't even remember most of them.

Our Christmas trees always reached the ceiling, with decorations galore. On Christmas mornings we would rush down to a room so filled with presents around the tree that we'd have to move the multitude simply to get to our stockings to begin our day.

I've always been small. Growing pains to get to my five-foot stature were hard, but proudly, by the time I was fourteen, I cleared the five-foot mark with an extra half an inch to spare. Despite this, the pile of presents around the Christmas tree always exceeded my height, no matter what age.

Despite all that excess during those years, I only remember a Barbie house, a bike, and a swing set. Probably because each of these offered me some type of escape from my life as I knew it.

My mother always went over the top. There was no middle road. Getting through Christmas was its own kind of madness.

She expressed her moments of depression with crying and absurd behavior. I'm sure that her self-medicating with excessive alcohol and, I suspect, prescription drug use, never helped. The crying and absurdity would lead to fits of rage; yelling and incessant screaming. I recall one time, she was so mad at my dad, that she went into our garage, grabbed a hammer and smashed his watch so hard and long that it pitted out the concrete.

As I mentioned a little while back, my mother was never officially diagnosed with anything at the time, but looking back, it's clear she struggled with extreme mental illness. I myself have suffered and been diagnosed with major depression during periods of my life. Others in my family have been diagnosed with different and similar severe mental diseases and in some cases a life sentence of disability. Given the genetic component, it's likely my mother had issues of bipolar depression with episodes of schizophrenia but in those days, seeing a psychiatrist was stigmatized, so it was all swept under the rug. We just accepted it as our normal.

Dissociation As a Survival Tool

I learned how to live in that environment. My dad always called me his "little trooper" and told me I was a survivor. Those were words I needed to hear and left me with a sense of needed approval, but what those formative years really taught me was how to disassociate from my body. As a result, throughout my life, right to today, I can endure a tremendous amount of pain, both physical and emotional. Even now, my few friends who have observed me in this state say they've never seen anything like it. I can completely detach my mind from my body, distancing myself from any intense or difficult reality unfolding around me. I'm sure those early years taught me how to do that. It's part of my tool chest now. Not always a good thing, but as a child, it was an essential survival strategy.

People ask if those early years impacted my own parenting, and it did. Of course, it did. It gave me a determination not to repeat the pattern and ingrained in me a deep desire to live differently.

I'm proud to say that it worked. I broke the pattern of abuse. My children have never been physically, mentally, or emotionally abused. Raising my girls, I used my father's method of discipline: he would tell us "no" once, then tell us "no" a second time sternly, and then if we pushed it, we'd get a spanking. But even when he spanked us, it was never in anger. It was calm, calculated, and deliberate. I can only remember my dad spanking me twice in my life.

It's funny how different that felt from my mother's beatings. She could (excuse the language) beat the shit out of me, and it didn't matter. I was numb to it like it didn't even register. But the few times my dad spanked me, it hurt—emotionally to my core more than physically.

Siloed

My middle sister suffered in her own way. Where I got most of the physical abuse, she got a lot of mental and emotional abuse.

Merina and I were different—she was more of a tomboy, and I was a girly girl. I loved playing with Barbies and spent a lot of time creating stories in my head. Before bed, I'd imagine tiny people climbing up my arms, living in a world I controlled. It was a way to self-soothe in a home where nothing made sense.

Merina was always chunky and a tomboy, and my mother was particularly cruel to her. She would tell her she was fat and ugly, even in public places like the pool, often in front of friends. The cruelty was so obvious that even their friends, years later, would ask how Merina was doing. People saw the meanness in my mother. She wasn't just harsh—her tongue was wicked. She said things that hurt our hearts.

The reality was she was a woman filled with anger and pain with no outlet other than to inflict that pain on others. She was self-absorbed and mean to everyone; every member of our family, her friends, and the people who helped her. But she was especially mean to herself. Her torment put her on a road that led nowhere but pain.

The dynamic between me and my sisters was a strange one. We were each born into a different phase of my parents' relationship. I was born when they were struggling. Merina was born when things were hard, but there was more financial stability. Arlington was born when my father's career was established and business was good.

I experienced the lion's share of physical abuse combined with emotional abuse, my middle sister took mostly emotional abuse, and my youngest sister was treated like a princess. It's as though we were three children living in three different worlds.

Our relationships were siloed. We were deliberately kept apart by my mother. I was the caretaker from a young age. As soon as I could reach the counter, I was making dinner, changing diapers, and taking on responsibilities far beyond my years. My mother was hands-on with Arlington, carrying her around like an accessory, dressed in perfect little outfits. Meanwhile, Merina and I were left to fend for ourselves.

Even though my middle sister and I were closer in age, we didn't play together much. We were so different. I played with my Barbies, and she spent time outside digging for worms. We lived separate lives, even when we were in the same house. My duties included making dinner and making sure we had food on the table. Arlington, meanwhile, was constantly with our mother, which left Merina alone a lot of the time.

Despite everything, I didn't feel resentment towards my sisters. Maybe there was some toward

Arlington because she was always treated so differently. We were kids, after all. Merina and I had our silly moments, like the time we made little ghosts out of Kleenex, drawing faces on them with a marker. We must have made 25 of them. We threw them into Arlington's room while she was in her nursery, and she started screaming for my mother. Merina and I rushed back in to pick up all the ghosts and acted like nothing had happened. It was harmless fun—nothing mean-spirited.

We did fight, though. There were definitely some knockdown, drag-out fights. Hair pulling, scratching, the usual sister stuff. I remember one time I got so fed up with Merina that I grabbed a bottle of baby powder and squirted it in her face. I got in trouble for that one, but honestly, it was probably deserved.

When the youngest was born, things did get easier for me and Merina. My mother's focus shifted to her, and some of the worst of the abuse let up. That's probably why there wasn't more resentment toward Arlington—her arrival brought a kind of relief for us. Things weren't as heavy as they had been before.

Looking back, there's no single memory that stands out from those early years. It's all blurred together in a way. I do remember feeling happy when other people were around—family and friends—because it made everything quieter in my head. The chaos would stop for a while.

I have general memories like my dad teaching me how to ride a bike on a dirt road so I wouldn't hurt myself if I fell. Or the times Merina and I played tennis in the backyard—me pretending to be Chrissie Evert and her as Billie Jean King. Those were the moments that felt normal.

But as soon as the door closed, the horror would begin again. Most people had no idea what went on behind those doors. My mother put on a perfect façade for the outside world.

A Shift

A quiet and unexpected shift happened when I was seven and got braces. It was a big deal for me. I had extra teeth, my mouth was a mess, and I had to wear headgear. It was a difficult time because I had been a thumb sucker—my one comfort—and the braces and headgear forced me to stop. Braces weren't common back then, and having headgear certainly wasn't considered cool. But in some way, that marked the beginning of a change for me, a transition from that small child into something more. It was nothing tangible, just an odd shift.

How I survived those years without breaking as a human being, I don't know. As children, we live on instinct, and what happens to us in those early years becomes the foundation of who we are. The choices we make, the chances we take, and how we handle the battles that rage inside us, all determine where we end up as adults. In the meantime, all we can do is survive the chaos day by day.

In my case, the impact of the chaos showed up in all sorts of unexpected ways, including sleepwalking and locking myself in bathrooms. My parents told me once that I'd got up in the middle of the night and they found me yelling at my closet door. Another time, I went downstairs and locked myself in the half-bathroom. I didn't remember any of it, but they found me there in the morning. I continued to sleepwalk through my twenties whenever life was particularly stressful and difficult.

Survival isn't always unconscious and instinctual. Art often comes out of struggle, and for me, that art was expressed in a children's book I wrote called *Garden of Peace*. It's a story about a little girl who lives in a world where animals, trees, and birds talk to her. It was just a hand-drawn book, but I kept it for over 30 years, maybe as a kind of quiet therapy for myself. A retreat into a world I could control.

My Dad

As for my father, not a lot changed. He worked, came home later, and we all simply survived on what was there. Mother rarely if ever made a home-cooked meal and never did laundry. We'd have to go to school with dirty clothes, pulling them out of a laundry room that was piled high—at least four feet tall. The room was about 8 by 10 feet, and it had two washers, but no one ever used them. He knew things weren't right. He knew there was chaos at home. He just didn't know what to do.

I think my father had his own struggles. He was driven by his career, and his goal was to make sure money was coming into the house. He was very focused, and as much as I love him, I know now that he must have felt burdened, maybe even trapped, by the situation with my mother. They fought a lot. At night we heard the continual arguing, often waking up to broken furniture and objects. This did not come from my father. Fierce with his words but he was and still is a very patient and controlled man.

I still remember one of their particularly violent fights. The morning after, we woke up to find one of our bar stools—this big, heavy piece of furniture—broken in half and thrown out with the trash. We'd heard my parents arguing the night before but didn't know what had happened until we saw the stool. It was clear my mother had broken it during the argument. It was one of those moments that stayed with me, and it was really just Merina and I who understood that we were looking at the result of my mother completely losing it. Arlington, being so young, had no idea what had happened.

Those stools seemed like bad luck.

Another time they caused a problem was when Arlington was just two years old, we came home from school to find her with her head wrapped in bandages. Mother was holding her in a recliner, and Dad was there, which was unusual. When we asked what happened, the story was that our mom had been sitting on one of the bar stools, talking with her friend, Priscilla—who we called Aunt Pris. Apparently, Arlington had been playing underneath the stool, and Mom fell off, landing on her. Arlington ended up needing major surgery, though thankfully not ocular surgery. She still has a scar from it.

"Those damn bar stools—nothing good ever seemed to come from them," my mother had said, claiming she was the victim in the incident.

Later we were to find out they had been drinking most of the afternoon. As she pushed away from the kitchen bar, she fell on top of my baby sister who was only crawling at this point in her life.

Despite it all, my dad stuck with the family unit. His work was demanding and he used it as an escape and a refuge. When he was around, he tried to engage with us, to create some sense of normalcy, but it was fleeting. It was hard on him to the degree that I remember times when he didn't come home at all, saying he was staying at the YMCA to work out and play handball. I think he just needed to get away from the house.

Looking back, I know my mother never wanted children. She simply utilized the opportunity to accomplish her own personal agenda: a perfect facade, the perfect little family, the perfect home, the lawyer husband.

The fact is, my dad had zero intentions of having children too. He shared with me many times that his intention after graduation from law school had been to go to Vietnam. It's hard to say that, but it's true. He has said that my birth changed the trajectory of his life. He has said that despite it all, it was changed in a good way. I have these memories of lying on his chest and falling asleep, and I know that he cared for me tenderly. I know that he has loved me from the beginning of my life till the end of our lives and I am forever gifted by this fact. But as the family expanded and the problems grew, it was easier for him to ignore what was happening at home and focus on his career.

In the end, I believe he didn't realize how bad things were. My mother made sure we kept our mouths shut, and we did. She never forgot or forgave any defiance. I've been beaten with the buckle end of a belt, scalded, and punched. Not just slaps and smacks. It was real abuse. But it was the life I was dealt, and I endured it.

What's strange is that I've come to accept it. I don't dwell on the negative. I don't sit around thinking about how I wasn't a wanted child. That's not a good feeling, and it's not something I like to focus on. But as I've grown, I've come to understand that I'm here for a reason, and there's a purpose to all of it.

I know this because of the thing that happened to me that strange night that changed the trajectory of my whole life.

I'm jumping forward a little, I hope you don't mind. I was about ten years old. I remember it vividly these 48 years later.

The Night That Saved Me

It was after a really bad day with my mom. My sisters and I were each in our own rooms, doors shut. I was in my room, crying, so distraught that I could hardly breathe. It was one of those days where the pain and confusion were overwhelming, and I remember sobbing uncontrollably.

At some point, through the tears, I asked out loud, "Why? Why does she hate me?"

Then something incredible happened. A light appeared in the corner of my room. It was a soft, calming hue of yellow, and it brought with it a sense of peace that washed over me. I didn't understand it at the time, but I wasn't scared. Moments later, at the end of my bed, another light appeared. It wasn't a human form, more like a vapor, but I knew instantly who it was. It was Jesus Christ.

You'd think, being a little girl, I would have been terrified of a figure in my room, but I wasn't.

I asked again, "Why does she hate me so much? Why?"

He spoke to me. He said, "Child, she knows not what she does. You are loved, and you always will be."

Then, just as He had appeared, He dissipated. The light in the corner faded, too, and I was left alone again.

You can believe it or not, but I've never questioned my faith since. That experience stayed with me, shaping who I would become.

I was in so much pain that day, feeling unloved, feeling worthless, and that manifestation saved me. It was a life-altering moment. I don't share this story with many people because it's so precious to me. I know not everyone believes in these things, and I respect that, but I was touched by God that day, and it changed the course of my life.

Over the years, I've had moments where I shouldn't have survived, but I know now that I have a purpose. I'm not afraid of dying, and I'm not afraid of the process of death, because I know what's waiting for me. When it's my time, I'll bow at His feet, kiss His feet, and thank Him for the love He showed me that day. That love has carried me through every chapter of my life.

I don't go around preaching or trying to convert people. My faith is personal, not about church or institutions, but about my own beliefs.

It took me a long time, but I've finally learned that you can't get that level of unconditional love from anyone else—not your parents, not your spouse, not your friends. You have to love yourself first. And that realization came from that experience so long ago.

We are all born perfect. It's society and life experiences that make us feel like we're not enough. I've lived through plenty of negativity, and I've made mistakes. But I've also learned that *positive in* yields *positive out*. It's something that's taken me decades to understand fully, but it all goes back to that moment when I was ten.

I didn't share that story with my sisters or anyone else at the time. We weren't a family that talked about things like that.

I did, however, for some reason I can't fathom, share it with my mother.

The Exorcist

It was the next morning. I was confused and wanted to make sure I hadn't imagined it.

"Child, she knows not what she does. You are loved, and you always will be," weren't the only words told to me by that visitation. He also told me that an aunt on my mother's side had passed and that my mother's anger would be misguided.

I told my mother what had happened and what I'd been told, and she reacted horribly. She called me a demon. She said I was possessed by evil and that I hadn't heard Jesus, but a voice from the other side—some distant aunt who had passed away. She was convinced I was hearing from this dead relative.

I remember asking, "Mom, do you have an Aunt Martha?"

She stopped and looked at me. "Yes, why?"

"Because she's died," I told her.

She brushed it off. "You don't know what you're talking about."

But later that afternoon, she got a call. Her Aunt Martha had passed away.

That moment only confirmed for her that I was evil. Around the same time, The Exorcist had come out, and she'd read the book and seen the movie with her friend. There were terrifying commercials on the television advertising the showing of this scary movie. As children, we would quickly change the channel as soon as we would hear the music. One night, after seeing the film with my Aunt Pris, she refused to come inside the house. She stood outside, yelling and screaming, convinced I was possessed like the character in the movie. I'm confident that she was intoxicated. My father had to coax her inside, and I remember standing in the hallway upstairs, hearing her shout that I was the girl from The Exorcist. My dad, who had come home from work, led her into their bedroom, but I'll never forget the look in her eyes. I believed, at that very young age, that my mother truly believed I was possessed. I was confused. My mother's behavior and response to what I'd said were beyond anything I'd witnessed or experienced before.

Faith

After that, I never spoke about it again—not with her, not with anyone, until decades later. Even now, only a few people know the full story. One of those people is my dad. He doesn't believe in anything spiritual—he calls himself an atheist, which is ironic considering he was the one who made sure we had structured religion in our lives growing up. He even studied at a seminary for a very brief period when he was young. After my parents got divorced, he flipped and started professing atheism, but I know deep down there's more to him than that.

My grandmother, his mother, was deeply faithful. She was my anchor and always told me, "As long as you have a mustard seed of faith, you will be accepted in God's kingdom." That stayed with me. I believe my dad has that mustard seed of faith, even if he doesn't realize it. He says what he says, but I know when his time comes, he'll see the truth, and I'll be happy for him.

When I did finally share the experience of that night with my dad, he didn't belittle it. He listened. He didn't agree, but he didn't dismiss it either. For me, this story is a powerful one because it speaks to the love I finally felt as a child—love I didn't get from my parents but from something higher. It opened me up to the idea of accepting love wherever I could find it, and that has stayed with me. I'm a hugger, a snuggler, and I always will be. That's how I connect with people, and it's a message I feel is so needed in this world.

Years later, when my mother passed, I didn't feel sad. I went to the funeral to comfort my sisters, but I wasn't mourning her. I felt grateful that she was no longer bound by the earthly demons she had carried. She lived her final days alone, bleeding out from alcohol in a hoarder's apartment. She died the way she lived—trapped. But I felt joy for her, knowing she was in a better place.

Those first seven years were hard, but they shaped me. They're part of the reason I am the way I am now. My softness, the way I deliver myself to the world, comes from those early struggles. Some people might brush it off, thinking their own childhood was tough, but it's all relative. When you've lived through something like this—through physical and emotional abuse, and then having a powerful experience with God at age 10 that was mocked and dismissed—it changes you.

After that night, something changed in me and because of it, I had a new sense of freedom. It didn't matter what my mom said anymore because I knew what was real. She would twist things, calling me evil or possessed, loser, worthless, ugly, useless, not wanted, a burden, stupid, a whore, but it didn't shake me. She was so busy with her social life that we were often pawned off on whoever would take us. In her chaos, I found a strange peace. I knew by then that she would never be a lighthouse or a beacon for me.

That was okay, though. I had my own lighthouse, my own beacon—and that was Jesus.

Transition

Between the ages of eight and fifteen, a shift happened for my family, both financially and socially. The move from the south side of St. Petersburg, where I had great childhood friends, to a new subdivision was good for us. It was a bigger house, and the Country Club with its tennis courts, my bike, and a new energy that naturally came with growing up little by little, gave me a sense of freedom and escape from the chaos of my family's dynamics.

This freedom also created more distance between me and my sisters. Being older, I had more privileges and my mother would do anything to not be burdened by us, which meant I could ride my bike to the club three miles away or go play tennis, which allowed me moments of relief from the madness at home. Those years felt quieter—not because they actually were, but because I had more choices than ever before. I could retreat into my own world inside that chaos, and it gave me a sense of control I hadn't known as a very young child.

At school, I was more active and part of different groups. My mother no longer had to pick us up, as we took the bus. In a way, this made those years feel quieter, too. It was a time when I was given opportunities to free myself from some of the control and turmoil.

It was also the time my parents built a pool in the backyard. I would spend hours in the water, testing how long I could hold my breath, relishing the silence it brought. It was an outlet, something I aspired to—a space to be free from the noise of life. Little did I know I'd stumbled on a solution to life that has served me ever since. I'll get to that in Part 2 of this book.

Finally, The Beatings Stopped

By this time, I was on the tennis team and becoming stronger. I had also put on some weight, as adolescents do.

Then, at fourteen, another moment changed the relationship between my mother and me.

We were preparing for a wedding, and I was in the bathroom when my mother, in a rage, came at me. But this time, I was strong enough to stop her. She swung to hit me, fists high, but I caught her hand mid-air and said, "If you lay another hand on me, I will kill you."

"If you lay another hand on me, I'll kill you."

It was something I had never imagined saying, but I'd reached a breaking point.

There was a moment's pause. She looked deep into my eyes, and I didn't flinch. My grip on her hand stayed firm. I could see she believed me. From that day on, she never hit me again.

Just because the physical abuse stopped, didn't mean the emotional or mental abuse got any less. It didn't. But things definitely became a little easier in that emotional and mental abuse was easier to cover up, so there were fewer questions at school.

Was I surprised at my actions?

Absolutely.

I didn't even know where the strength came from. My mom was strong, especially on the tennis court. She was competitive, and she'd wear me out when we played. So, to suddenly have the strength to hold her back—it came out of nowhere. I still don't know how I did it, but I'm grateful I did.

I do regret the words I said to her that day. They were harsh, but they were the only words I could think of to stop the violence. I was tired—tired of the chaos, tired of being beaten down, both physically and emotionally. The yelling didn't faze me, but the physical beatings had worn me out.

That moment of rage was the only time I've ever said anything like that to anyone. I'd never reached that boiling point before, and I haven't since. But at that moment, I needed to stop her.

Even though the yelling and screaming didn't stop, the physical abuse did. At last, the beatings were over.

It's strange, talking about it now. I don't feel emotional about it anymore. It's like I've become detached, like I'm telling someone else's story. I can remember it all, but the emotion isn't there.

That was the beginning of my shelling. I started building layers of protection, creating a shell around myself. I learned to smile while hiding the pain I was going through. No one knew what was really happening inside.

I'll tell you that in my late twenties, I did meet with my mother to talk about forgiveness but even so, there was no relationship left to salvage. I've moved on from it—not in the sense of repairing anything, but in finding peace within myself.

Forgiveness, for me, has been about self-acceptance.

It's difficult, though, because I'm still so critical of myself, even today. I know I was just a child, and logically I get that, but emotionally, it's hard not to be hard on myself. What could I possibly have done differently? Why would I need to forgive myself when I didn't choose to be in that situation?

I've come to terms with the fact that I was just surviving. My life was profoundly shaped by mental illness—particularly my mother's struggles. It's something I had no control over. She had always been troubled, and as a child, I couldn't fully understand that. I've forgiven her for what she couldn't control, and I've learned not to place blame on myself for things I had no power over. It took me a long time to accept that my childhood wasn't something I could have changed.

But there's one thing I still struggle with—the words I said in a moment of desperation. I can't seem to let go of that. Those words have stayed with me for so long, almost as if I'm holding onto them too tightly.

"If you touch me again, I'll kill you."

Those words—they feel like they belong in some compartment of my past, but I don't know if I've really been able to put them away. Maybe because you can't erase moments like that. They linger. I know those words came from a place of survival, not from the person I truly was or am today. But at that moment, it was about protecting myself. Today, my heart is completely filled with love, there's no anger, and it's never entered my head to harm anyone. It's still hard to reconcile those words, but I needed to survive.

At that time, my mother's condition was getting worse. Her behavior became more unpredictable, and I was constantly on edge, never knowing what would come next.

There was a particular day that stood out to me. She didn't direct her anger at me, but I watched as she took out her frustration on objects around her. She was lost in her own world of pain, and I was just trying to stay out of the way. I remember thinking, "I can't keep living like this." It was survival in its most basic form.

And survive I did.

Around that time, though, my middle sister didn't have the same freedoms I did. My youngest sister, the "Princess," was content at home, but my middle sister seemed stuck, and that's when she and the youngest bonded more. They developed a closer relationship, even though it's not as strong today. I was always the one left out. They had a bond that I didn't share, and I was often alone in that. But honestly, I didn't mind.

Alone, But Not Lonely

When I think about it now, I was always alone, but I never felt lonely.

Merina, closest in age to me by 21 months, was always crying for my dad and she would cling to him as soon as she saw him. Considering my mother's behavior, this wasn't unexpected. But it made her a difficult child to handle. My mother couldn't manage her at all, but my dad sometimes got through to her.

I adored my dad, so seeing him struggle with her hardened my relationship toward her. I was a young child who got no love from my mother and saw my father as my lifeline. The more he had to focus on Merina, the less time he had for me. That's how I saw it at the time.

Years later, I spoke to Merina about our childhood, and she explained how my parents divorce when I was around 15 and she was 14 just about crushed her.

I'll get to the full story in a bit, but suffice to say, Dad knew the legalities of divorce well and knew that children would be awarded full custody to the mother. I was at the age of consent in Florida, so refused to stay with my mother, and went with my dad. This left both my sisters in a house of chaos without me or my dad for protection. Merina saw Dad as her savior. She said she's never gotten over his abandonment and has never been able to forgive him.

It was just another layer that created that sense of separation between me and them. I was the one who managed to escape my mother first. I got to leave with my dad. None of this was easy for my sisters.

As I said, I was always alone, but never lonely. Although I'm grateful I never felt lonely, the feeling of being alone frequently took breath from my body.

To protect myself from that sense of isolation, I spent years hardening and building my walls and outer shell so I didn't have to feel the pain I felt as a child. That shell served me well for years. It was my shield of protection. My heart from the beginning was so tender, and I felt loss and lack, hurt and betrayal unimaginably deeply.

Part of my defense was to be as perfect as I could be. So much so, that people called me "Little Ms. Sarah Bernhart". My life was an act. I lived every day like I was playing a part:

professionally trained from birth to pretend and be what I perceived others wanted to see from me. It served its purpose, but there was a price. No one could break through to the heart. I absorbed love like a lifeline, but it never felt entirely safe.

Being able to truly love was a hard lesson to learn, but I learned this lesson the day I dropped the shield to allow the love of my life to know me. Not the fragments of what the character I'd created was, but all of me.

The journey to this freedom hadn't even begun. I didn't know that one day, I'd take a massive leap of faith. I had no idea that the sense of being utterly alone would one day be filled with more love than I could imagine. It's a love I lost after just 17 years. Of all my losses, that one literally took the breath from my body.

But that story is yet to come. Right now, I was just learning my body and understanding what growing up meant for a young girl.

With that said, the first time I was truly aware of my body was a shock.

The Mistake That Triggered a Lifelong Struggle

As I mentioned in our early years, even though my middle sister didn't suffer the same physical abuse, she endured emotional torment. She was chunky and chubby and was called awful names—fatso, worthless, lazy.

Every night, we said goodnight to our parents, and I remember one night, as I hugged my dad, he said, "Good night, Merina."

He didn't say, "Goodnight, Michelle." He said Merina.

My heart sank. He had confused me with my sister.

Now, I know it wasn't intentional, but at the time, it felt like a dagger to my heart.

Around that time, I had gained some weight, not a lot, but to me, it felt massive.

How could my dad have mistaken me for Merina? Was I really chunky, chubby, fatso, worthless, and lazy?

That was all it took. Those few words at the end of a day before bed. That tiny mistake that my dad didn't even notice. That was the moment that spiraled me into anorexia.

It wasn't malicious on my dad's part. It was just a mix-up, exhausted from his day, but given my mindset and my lack of control over my life, it felt devastating. I couldn't control anything else. What I could control was what went into my body.

It started when I was around fourteen. During dinner, instead of eating, I'd go swimming. My eating habits went mostly unnoticed. At school, I had friends who struggled with the same issues, which only reinforced my behavior.

Since then, my weight has always been an issue, both gaining and losing. When I felt unsafe, I'd gain weight; when I felt like I had no control,

I'd lose it. It became a cycle tied to my emotional state.

It wasn't good for me. It became a battle I'd fight my whole life, but it was also a turning point.

I had found a way to feel in control.

A struggle with weight is something all us girls struggle with. We're all self-conscious about it. It's part of our family dynamic, part of the image we were taught to value. The physicality of beauty. Even now, after losing a hundred pounds, that inner struggle remains. The weight comes on and the weight goes off. It's something I recognize when I fall into those patterns. It still remains a work in progress for me—like my weight is never good enough.

So, a lot happened around fourteen years old. The anorexia began, and my mother stopped hitting me. I had also become comfortable with the idea that the love I received from others was enough. Like I said before, I soaked it up—soaked it up from my dad, from my grandma. My grandma, his mother, was like a second mom to me, even though she lived all the way in Pensacola, ten hours away. I'd spend summers with her. They'd put me on a plane, and I'd go stay for a few weeks at a time. She was a home economics teacher, and she was such an incredible woman. She loved me deeply as I loved her deeply.

As I got older, especially in my twenties, I'd talk to her every single day. "Hey, Grandma, what's going on?" She was like my best friend. She taught me how to crochet, how to knit—all the fun things we did together. She loved me enough to just be there with me. Merina and Arlington didn't have that kind of relationship with her, though. That connection was mine alone.

We also had a neighbor, who lived right next door. She was kind to me and everyone. When I wanted to move my furniture around in my bedroom, my mother refused to help, but this neighbor came over and helped me rearrange it. I found other avenues of kindness, other loving actions from people around me, and that sustained me. It fueled me and reminded me that everything was going to be okay.

Until it wasn't.

Life Shifting and Altering

At fifteen, another huge turning point hit our family. To give you the backstory...

By now, my dad had started to drift away emotionally from the family. I think he had been worn down by it all. Around the time things were at their worst, he fell in love with this kind neighbor. Her name was Marian. She was always around because we lived next door, and our families spent a lot of time together.

At some point, my dad and Marian developed a bond. They were both in difficult marriages, and I guess they found comfort in each other. Looking back, it all makes sense, though at the time, I didn't really understand it. My mother, on the other hand, was spiraling, engaging in destructive behavior that made our home unbearable. My dad had found a way out—emotionally, at least—by getting close to Marian. Meanwhile, I was still there, trying to make sense of everything.

Our neighbor's family was a mess, too. My mother had inappropriate relationships within Marian's family, which only added to the chaos. But despite all of this, there was something real between my dad and Marian. There was genuine love for each other, and even after we moved, their relationship continued. I didn't resent Marian—I was actually happy for my dad. She was a good person, and in many ways, she was probably the escape he needed.

But as with everything in our family, good things never came easy.

Don't Look Back, Honey

So, with all that going on in the background, my mother and father got into another fight; it wasn't anything new; they fought all the time. But this time, she left. She took off to St. Petersburg Beach and stayed in a suite on the top floor of the Hilton, right on the water. She was gone for almost a month.

Living in a house without her was pure peace. For the first time in our lives, we had organization.

While she was gone, my dad had all the laundry done. We had clean clothes, we had dinner, and for the first time, we had a routine. We knew what needed to be done. There wasn't any loudness, no yelling. Life was peaceful.

Then, one day, I came home, and my mother was in the kitchen—cooking. I remember calling my dad at his office. "Dad, Mom's here... she's cooking dinner." There were no cell phones.

He told me, "It's okay, honey. Don't worry about it. I'm on my way." He made it home within the hour.

When he arrived, everything was all nicey-nice, but it felt off. Eventually, he took her out of the house—maybe to talk somewhere away from us girls or something. When he came back, my dad sat us down on the couch. He was in the middle, Merina was on one side, Arlington on the other, and I sat next to Arlington. He explained that Mom was moving back home and that they would be getting a divorce.

It was the first time I ever saw my father cry.

We were all crying. I remember telling him, "I'm going with you. All of us, we're going with you." But as a lawyer, he knew that custody law almost always went to the mother. Still, I was at an age where my voice could be heard.

I didn't give him a choice. "You take me, or I'm leaving. I don't know where I'm going, but I'm not staying here."

I think, by that age, I'd developed enough gumption, a little teenage sass, and I wasn't going to back down. I told him, "I'm not staying. I'm going with you."

And he let me.

Merina and Arlington stayed behind with my mother. I remember the day we left, driving away in the morning.

As we pulled out of the driveway, my dad said, "Don't look back, honey, just don't look back."

It was hard—really hard—not to look back.

"Why did my dad say, 'Don't look back'?" I don't know. Maybe he thought it would be hurtful or upsetting to me. The whole experience was upsetting, so maybe he was trying to protect me. Maybe it was his way of saying, "Let's move forward."

For me, it had a lot of meaning. It was a life lesson captured in a few words. It's something I've carried with me—*always moving forward*. I reflect, sure, but I don't dwell on the past. I learn from it, then move on.

That night, my dad and I had dinner together, and the next day, we went to St. Pete Beach. My dad found a condo for us to stay in for the summer. I turned sixteen while we were there—my birthday's July second.

"Happy birthday," you might say. I would say thank you. But my sweet sixteen wasn't what you might imagine.

Freedom and the Trouble It Brings

At home with my mother, we were allowed to play in the neighborhood, but always with strict oversight. When I moved in with my dad, all the structure disappeared. He didn't really have any boundaries, so I went from a very controlled life to sudden freedom.

That kind of freedom is overwhelming for any teenager, and it was no different for me. Suddenly, I was driving for the first time and making decisions on my own. I'll never forget the first time I drove by myself.

I was at the beach. I remember driving around, turning up the radio, and enjoying the freedom.

My dad had this massive blue Lincoln Continental, and since I was so small, it looked like no one was driving. I had the radio on, and I heard a "woo, woo, woo" sound. I panicked, thinking I was being pulled over. I pulled the car over, put it in park, and sat there for ten minutes, waiting. Eventually, I realized the sound was coming from a song on the radio, not a police siren. That's how nervous I was.

That car became a bit of a joke. My high school had this long road that led to the gym, and people would line up in the mornings to watch "the blue boat" roll in—because from the outside, it looked like no one was driving it.

During that time, I was navigating new freedoms but also a lot of confusion. My dad didn't impose many rules. I remember actually asking him for a curfew because all my friends had one. He asked what I thought it should be, and we settled on 11 PM. That was the end of the discussion. It felt freeing to have so much independence, but it also left me vulnerable. I didn't know how to handle certain situations, especially when it came to boys and older men.

The Trouble With Men

Physically, I was small in stature but large-breasted, which drew attention from not just boys, but men—sometimes even my dad's friends. I had no idea how to handle that. Mentally, I still felt like a little girl, and the attention was overwhelming and confusing. That confusion, along with everything else I was dealing with, contributed to my struggle with anorexia. I felt lost, alone, and like I had no one to guide me through these experiences.

My dad did his best to support me. He even took me to my first gynecology appointment and tried to be there for me in ways most fathers wouldn't. But he was also running a law practice, so I had to figure out a lot on my own.

During this time, I had a kind of sexual awakening, though it wasn't as dramatic as that sounds. I didn't lose my virginity until I was almost 17, and it was with my high school boyfriend. We had a promise ring and went to church together. I thought we were going to get married.

That experience was actually a positive one. I had heard horror stories from friends about their first times, but mine wasn't like that. It was real and honest.

As I got older, though, curiosity got the better of me. After high school, I wanted to see what else was out there, and that led to our breakup. He was a good guy—older but a little immature. My dad welcomed him into our home, and for a high school relationship, it was a positive experience.

But outside of that relationship, things were more difficult.

In one instance, I was in a hotel elevator, and an older man tried to kiss me and grope me. I didn't know how to handle it. I committed to surviving the moment and waited for the door to open so I could escape. I never reported or confronted anyone about these incidents; I just tried to get away. At the time, that's just what women did.

I started working as a receptionist when I was 18, and one of my first jobs was at a T-shirt imprint shop. The VP of sales there made aggressive advances toward me. It got too much and I eventually quit that job because of it. I moved on to another job, working as an assistant for two VPs at a marine company. There was an investor who would call me often. It started off as harmless, flirty conversation, but when he visited the office, he pursued me in a way that made me uncomfortable.

I wasn't interested, but he didn't take no for an answer. It got to the point where he started stalking me. He would call and say things like, "I can see you cooking. What are you making for dinner?" It was incredibly unsettling. Eventually, my boyfriend at the time, who later became my first husband, threatened him, and the man backed off.

It was during this time I was raped by a guy at a party that I attended. This same guy came into the condominiums where I lived. He had an open invitation with a group of other "friends" and proceeded to rape me again. I was confused and figured it was my fault, like I was asking for it. I have never shared this story, simply because of the shame. And especially since the victims in such cases are all too often treated like the perpetrator.

I'm sharing it now because my desire to help others means I must be open and vulnerable. The shame over this horrific experience still sits heavy on my heart. The details are fragmented and tormenting at the same time. I don't think I'm alone in how this feels. The personal and societal judgment as I put myself in that position was and remains very strong. This is one of those memories I've tucked away in my mental library.

From that day forward, I am, and have always taught my girls, to be aware of their surroundings, and not be comforted by a false sense of security. There are people in the world who simply do horrible things to others.

Years later, I found out that this same man had been arrested in California for drugging and assaulting women. The police found tapes of his crimes, and he's still in prison. It was shocking to learn how dangerous he had been, and it's chilling to think I could have been one of his victims.

That wasn't the last time I had to handle abusive men. After leaving the marine company, I took a job at a pediatric dentist's office. The work environment wasn't great there either. The dentist was rude to his staff, vile toward women, and treated his wealthier patients very differently from those who were less well-off. He would offer free services to his rich friends but would demand payment from lower-income families who desperately needed help. I couldn't stand working in that kind of environment, so I left and found a job selling copiers at Danka. That marked the beginning of a new chapter in my life.

But I'm jumping the gun. Let me back up a little.

Body Issues

Through this time (finishing school, learning about men, navigating my first jobs), I plunged deeply into anorexia. My lowest weight then was probably around eighty-two pounds. I'm only five feet tall, had a large chest, and I remember wearing a bikini and feeling completely out of place.

I'd been living a controlled life, and suddenly, there were no boundaries. Men and boys were hitting on me, and I had no idea how to navigate it all. I remember sitting out on the patio, looking out over the water, and just rocking, feeling completely overwhelmed by life.

With no one to turn to or talk to, I just kept working things out. There was no other choice.

My instinct at the time was to seek out silence. The noise of life can be overwhelming, and since I'm sensitive to it, I found that sitting in stillness and breathing through events enabled me to quiet the chaos and organize what I needed to do or not do to move forward.

As I got better at calming my mind, I started to gain a more reasonable amount of weight. That happened just before school started that year, and we moved to downtown St. Petersburg.

My dad and I lived in a condo there, just the two of us for about five months until one day, he got a call from my mother.

Sisters Together Again

He had just had surgery and was recovering, but without notice or reason, my mother chose to kick Merina and Arlington out of the house. Locked them on the front porch, and put all their toys and clothes in garbage bags for my father to pick them up.

I can't imagine the torment they must have experienced at her hands during their time with her. It couldn't have been good. We never have spoken about it. The feeling of being tossed out like garbage to be disposed of must have made them feel horrible.

My dad went to pick them up from our old family home. They moved in and lived with us from that point forward. Feeling the pressure, my dad called my grandma and asked her to come down from Pensacola for a period in the transition. Thankfully, with joy, she agreed.

That period of time was a huge transition. I wasn't thrilled about suddenly having to take on more responsibilities, the ones I thought I'd finally been freed from. But we did the best we could.

We stayed at our rented condominium for about a year, and then my dad bought a three-story townhouse downtown, St. Petersburg. Dad had the third-floor bedroom, my sisters had the large bedroom on the second floor, and I had the loft on the same floor.

Living in the loft sucked as a teenager. I had no privacy, and I could hear everything going on in the house. But it worked for the time.

At sixteen, I went to the same private school I'd been attending since kindergarten. My graduating class only had fifty-eight students, so it wasn't a big school. My sisters went there for a time, too. We did normal teenage things and for a while, it was good.

When I turned seventeen, life took its next turn.

Teenage Problems

I was in a car accident—a fatal one. This is what happened...

I was a new driver on a frequently traveled one-way street. Being a quiet part of town, late at night, the lights were timed to turn as you approached.

My friend was driving his car. With the music on loud, we jockeyed back and forth down this road.

When the light turned, my friend got to it first and cleared the intersection. Behind him, I placed my foot on the gas pedal because I'd slowed on my initial approach to the changing light.

As my car accelerated across the intersection, there was an explosion of noise and everything suddenly seemed to fall into slow motion.

I could see a truck through the windshield spinning clockwise in rotation and then flipping over and over again and then just suddenly STOP!

Looking through the windshield there was smoke coming out of my engine in front of me. The truck was upside down and gasoline was pouring out of it.

I don't even know how I started to walk towards the truck. I was in a daze. There were beer bottles everywhere smashed on the street. I couldn't work out where all the glass had come from. I heard nothing. I just walked towards the truck and looked inside. On the ground, hanging halfway from inside the truck on the passenger side, I saw a person. The horror was beyond imagination; blood everywhere. I stood there, just looking, not moving and not having any clue about what just happened.

Two people walked me away from the truck to a corner, and I simply collapsed.

The ambulances came, police sirens, lights everywhere.

I do remember, while they had me in the ambulance, they asked, "Young lady, have you had anything to drink tonight?"

I said, "Well, I had my mom's sherry-cherry jello."

Now, I realize that wasn't what they were asking. They were asking about those beer bottles. Much later, I was told that the beer had come from a cooler in the back bed of the truck involved.

The passenger, a young mother, was killed. She hadn't been wearing a seatbelt, and the truck rolled over her head and body when she fell from the passenger window. I hadn't been wearing a seatbelt either which is why I cracked my car windshield with my head.

Once again, it was one of those unimaginable events that should have killed me, but I believe that God or an angel, for some reason, held me back from being ejected from my own car.

The accident and the death of that woman impacted me hugely. I could not sleep for months. The guilt, the images, the event. I was terrified of being alone. If my dad had to leave, I literally kept all the lights on and remained awake.

The image, that woman's death, has haunted me forever. I still say a prayer for her family to this day.

The accident was deemed as not my fault. My friend had already cleared the intersection on a green light prior to me entering it. The truck had run the red light.

All of my teenage challenges were causing my dad to step back from keeping his practice alive and thriving. More guilt and shame on me. Add to that, he was now managing three girls at home and was newly divorced from my mother. It was a lot for him.

Around this time, he met my stepmother-to-be.

Love Isn't Always Enough

She was a spicy, good-looking entertainer with no interest in having children, or being a mother. Despite all he had on his plate, she was interested in him. He, on the other hand, wasn't interested in marriage. She was okay with that, and they dated for twenty-five years before they finally tied the knot.

She was a good woman and put up with more than she could have ever bargained for being with him and three teenage girls.

They were together for over forty years before her death. The love and patience that she gave to my dad and our whole family earned her a special place in my heart.

My sisters were never nice to her. Ever. Even after everything she did for us. It was hurtful.

My youngest sister especially, simply couldn't accept her. Frankly, no one would ever have been welcomed by them.

I always appreciated and loved her for what she brought to my dad's life. It was okay that she wasn't maternal, not all women are that way. I loved her for the love that she gave to my dad and the love my dad still has for her today. You can imagine what she had to put up with; three demanding teenage girls all broken by the past. All acting out in different ways.

The Last Straw!

Teenage problems with Merina always loomed large but were now on steroids! Things really fell apart when my father took a ski trip to Austria.

I was put in charge of caring for my two younger sisters. With my dad away, Merina rebelled like most teenagers do; going out with friends, stealing street signs, toilet papering houses…things like that. Then she skipped school and went to my mother's house, took all the liquor she could carry and ended up hanging out with a bad group of people. She drank so much that she had to be rushed to hospital with alcohol poisoning.

With my dad away, my mom ended up coming to the hospital with all the drama of playing her part as the concerned mother. Since she no longer had custody rights, the hospital wouldn't release Merina into her care. I had no rights as Merina's 18-year-old sister because she was a minor. We had no choice: the call to my Dad had to happen. He wasn't happy. He had to return from the ski trip to deal with it.

His answer was to get us all home and send us to our rooms.

I was angry. I'd handled everything while he was gone, and now he was sending me to my room like a child? I thought, "I've done all this, and now you're punishing me?"

I felt so cheated. My whole existence was always about caring for my sisters, cleaning up after everyone, making sure all of us got to where we needed to go. Then Dad goes off skiing while I have to deal with all the drama with Mom at the hospital? It wasn't fair. I was a child but I was also a grown-up when it worked for everyone else.

So, feeling angry and betrayed, I decided to sneak out and meet my boyfriend. It was the only time I ever snuck out of the house. Unlike my sister Merina, I was always the rule follower. Never giving any real lip or resistance to rules or demands of responsibility.

My sisters knew I'd snuck out, and they chose to stuff my bed with pillows to make it look like I was still there.

Then they did something that perhaps they thought would just be a bit of fun - or maybe not. They ran upstairs to Dad and said, "Dad! Michelle's not responding! Something's wrong!"

He came rushing to my room, only to find it filled with pillows instead of me.

When I got home later that night, I thought I was in the clear. Dad didn't say anything. But at 7:30 the next morning, he woke me up.

"Michelle, pack your stuff. You're out of the house."

I was stunned. "You've got to be kidding me," I said to my dad.

"I'm not kidding. Pack it all. You're out. You're eighteen. You can make decisions, and you think you can make the decision to go out and do what you want when I've told you what you're supposed to do. So, pack it up," he said.

From that day forward, I never lived with my dad again—until now, when he's living in my house. Funny how life works.

That same day, I found myself homeless. I was shocked. I was hurt. I was angry. My head was spinning so fast that I had no idea what I was going to do. At first I thought he was just mad and would get over it. That didn't happen.

Homeless

During that time, I was still going to junior college. I couch-surfed for a bit, then slept in my car for about three months, using the facilities at the college to shower. I was so scared at night, I figured I would park in neighborhoods, but police officers would often knock on my car window, waking me up and telling me to move along.

I was scared to death, alone, with no real friends as their parents had told them not to get involved. I was, however, a stubborn survivor facing life day by day simply trying to hang on with no roadmap to follow.

Yes, I wanted to go back home, but I was also putting my foot down. I was tired of the years I spent having to be an adult when I was simply a child. No way was I going back to ask for forgiveness for such a small infraction.

Years before and years later, I always thought my sisters were given so much more of my dad's time, money, and attention. They never had the same expectations put on them that I did.

I tried staying at my mother's house for a while, but it didn't take long for the chaos to resurface. She was verbally abusive as always, and one morning, I woke up to find her trying to pull my boyfriend out of bed so she could seduce him. That's how it was with her—she had sexual relationships with men throughout my childhood, even some of my friends.

At that time, I was working a part-time retail job and barely scraping by. I wrote a bad check for $60 at a store, which ended up being a huge mistake. In Florida, writing a bad check over $50 was considered a felony. I didn't realize the seriousness of it until a friend told me the police were looking for me. Honestly, this wasn't the first time. It was something I would do on a pretty regular basis when I was really desperate and needed gas, food, or other items. The checks were linked to an account my dad had opened for me. He put my allowance in there. Well, when he kicked me out, the allowance stopped. The naive child in me figured I'd write the checks and Dad would cover it. He didn't.

Soon enough, the police showed up at my mother's house and arrested me. I was terrified. They took me to the county jail, not the city jail, which was where the really bad criminals went as it was the weekend. The officers were kind enough, though. They handcuffed me in the front, not the back, and even let me sit in the front seat of the car.

At the county jail, my dad refused to post bail. My friends and my mom eventually came up with the bond money, but it took hours before I was released. I was in a solid jail cell, all by myself, with just a small opening in the door. I was too scared to say anything, but after being there so long, I mustered up enough courage to ask an officer a question. I was ignored. They just passed by without acknowledging me. Or maybe I just was so scared my voice couldn't be heard over all the clamoring.

"Sir, could you please keep my door open? It's very dark in here."

Then one of the officers finally said, "We're doing this for your protection as much as anything else."

They didn't want anyone to hurt me, and being isolated was their way of keeping me safe.

And so, I talked myself into being alright with it all, saying things like, "I don't mind. I'm alone. I'm not lonely."

I didn't get out until twelve hours later. Everything that I'd said to myself was simply crap. I did mind, I was alone, I was lonely. My life was a complete mess. I had no idea what to do with myself.

Growing Up and Working Things Out

After that, I was put into a program called Pretrial Intervention. Since I didn't have any prior offenses, I was allowed to complete probation, and then everything would be expunged from my record. I'll never forget the parole officer telling me, "Oh yeah, they all say that. You'll be back in three months."

"Hello!" I thought. "That's not going to be me."

That experience was a wake-up call. Afterward, I went to my dad and told him, "Dad, I need a roof over my head."

He agreed to give me $300 a month, which was just enough for a place in the worst part of town. I lived in an efficiency apartment, but I couldn't afford the electricity. I had an extension cord plugged into an outlet outside the building, and I used it to power a single lamp, which I'd move around the apartment depending on where I needed light. The bathroom and kitchen had no power, but the water was included, so I made do.

I was learning how to live on my own and deal with the realities of adult life. It took a while, but eventually, I saved up enough to move into a studio apartment and get the lights turned on. It felt like a huge accomplishment. Learning to pay bills, take care of myself, and manage the responsibilities of adulthood was part of my growth during that time.

But even as I tried to establish myself, I still faced challenges, especially when it came to men crossing boundaries. I didn't know how to say no. I didn't know when to say no. I didn't know I could.

Despite the difficulties, that period of my life was about figuring out who I was and gaining the independence I needed to move forward.

At that time, I was living in rough areas, and I had some unsettling experiences. For instance, I knew the spokesperson for the St. Petersburg Police Department because I worked at a gym for a while. He was very aggressive towards me, especially sexually. There were times when we'd end up alone in an office, and suddenly, he'd try to kiss me, even though he had a girlfriend or wife. He once showed up at my door—because he was with the police, he knew where I lived—and asked me to be his mistress, saying he would pay for everything. I told him that wasn't going to happen.

These situations were demoralizing and disparaging. They made me feel like men were seeing me like a piece of property. It was strange. Maybe because I looked mature, or perhaps it was the vibes I unknowingly gave off?

The horrible role model in my mother and the things that I had witnessed during my childhood did not give me any foundation to deal with such things.

I guess I have to take some responsibility. In those days, I didn't know how to navigate those situations. I was people-pleasing, so these men might not have heard me say no.

I'd never before or since had someone just show up at my door like that. I think being young, naive, and unaware contributed to what I went through—especially when it came to getting into an abusive relationship with my first husband. I just didn't know any better, and I didn't have a "normal" life experience to fall back on. I had nothing inside of me to say or know, "This isn't right." I didn't know anything about self-worth and had never had a healthy role model of what a relationship between a man and a woman should be like. I was working things out as I went and making a lot of mistakes.

When I think of what I learned during this time, I don't think I learned any real lessons. At least not the kind that gave me a foundation for a healthy relationship. My relationship with my high school sweetheart was more like puppy love—boyfriend-girlfriend stuff but without any depth. His parents were around, my dad was around, but it was just surface-level.

Even with my experiences with other men. I never got a solid structure for understanding what a real relationship looked like. I'd never witnessed one as a child, and I didn't have any mentors or role models to show me what a good relationship should be.

If anything, I'd say the biggest lesson I learned through that time was the importance of finding your tribe—people who can be mentors, and who have positive experiences to share.

I didn't know what that tribe would look like because I hadn't ever had one. I call it a tribe now, but at that time, it was really about knowing what a functional family looked like for me.

And that's important. We need guidance from others to help us navigate relationships. We need that guidance from the right people. And if they aren't already in your family circle, you need to find them. There are people who will support and genuinely guide you, not judge or shame you. You must take each experience without self-judgement, learn from it, and pivot so you head in your right direction.

I had no roadmap. There was no book or guide for me to follow, and even if there was, I probably wouldn't have been interested at that time. I was so overwhelmed by life. I made a lot of mistakes, we all make mistakes and are flawed, but that doesn't define where we're at or where we're going.

You Get to Choose

You have the power to make changes, even if those changes aren't perfect at first. You can always pivot and make another change to get onto the right path. You must continue the movement of change. Always!

Life has a way of teaching us through consequences. As you grow, you absorb those lessons, and they stay with you forever. You can't control the actions of others, but you can control your own choices. This is everyone's superpower! You get to choose and take action for change. Even when those choices aren't perfect, they're right for you in that moment, and they can be stepping stones to something better. The key is to not get stuck. Don't let yourself sink into the dark places. You can't escape your difficulties through overindulging in food, self-harm, harm to others, gambling, sex, drugs or alcohol. I had to learn how to recognize when things were wrong and say no. Hiding from the issues your upbringing left you with won't solve your problems. You only postpone dealing with it.

What you go through becomes part of your life story. It's important to acknowledge where you've been, where you are, and where you're going. You don't want to go back to those dark times. They pass, but you can't stay stagnant. You have to keep moving forward and making changes, even if they feel small or imperfect. Sleeping in my car, for example, wasn't perfect, but it was a step up from moving back into my abuser's house. Take action. Move forward, even if it's just a bit. Just don't stay in the wrong place.

It's not easy. Especially if you've come from a background of abuse. Until you learn that abuse isn't normal, it's hard to make better decisions and set boundaries.

My first marriage was to an abuser. I didn't have strong boundaries. I hadn't learned to stand up for myself, and instead of learning that lesson, I went for what I was used to. This all happened partly because I was a people-pleaser. I wanted to make everyone around me happy, so I didn't focus on what I wanted or needed.

When I say people-pleaser, I mean that I had been conditioned my whole life, to my very core, to be exactly that! I pleased people to my own detriment. I did what made them happy at my pain and expense. On the other hand, pleasing others in a way that keeps your boundaries intact and brings joy to everyone is the right way to live life. The problems come when you deny yourself while keeping everyone else happy.

For Once, In My Favor

That being said, not having those boundaries ultimately led me to stumble into a job at Danka, where I took the copier sales job. I truly believe it was part of God's plan, not mine. If I had been like many in today's generation—setting strict boundaries about what I would accept, what I thought I deserved, and what I was willing to do—I might not have taken that job. But because I didn't have those boundaries, I worked incredibly hard. If they told me to make 100 calls a day, I made 100 calls, plus more. I was eager to please my managers and the executives. I was all about doing what was expected of me and more, which ultimately worked out in my favor. It provided me with stability, a professional skill set, knowledge, a commitment to succeed and so much more.

Interestingly, my hiring manager at Danka was a woman, and she was a total badass. Up until that point, I had only worked for men, so this was a significant change. That shift in working for a strong woman helped mark the beginning of a new chapter in my life.

Looking back, I wish I had created more boundaries, but in some ways, not having them allowed me to grow and learn. Today's generation sometimes seems too quick to set limits on what they're willing to do. If the pay or the hours aren't exactly what they want, they walk away. They don't seem to recognize the value of foundational training. And that can hold them back emotionally, financially, and professionally.

You have to experience things to gain wisdom. That's how you educate yourself and grow. If I had drawn hard lines back then, I might have missed out on the opportunity to really prove myself and grow into the person I became.

Part of that growth included my first marriage.

My First Marriage

I met Don when I was 18. We dated for seven years and got married when I was 25.

It was a physical attraction. Bodybuilding was all the rage during that time—think Muscle Beach in California. Don was a bodybuilder, and that made me feel safe. After dealing with being stalked, having a man like Don around made me feel protected.

He was my age, and we met at a bar in the Gulfport Beach area. It might have been the same bar, or maybe it had a different name, but it was the same place where my parents had met. It was a happening spot back then. I was friends with another bodybuilder, and they introduced me to him. I was immediately interested.

Don lived with his parents, and I had my own efficiency apartment, so we weren't living together. His parents were nice enough, but they weren't particularly warm. His dad was much older and Cuban, while his mom was German. Don's dad was the head of the household, and his mom had more of a passive role. They didn't have a lot of money, and it wasn't a close family unit.

Don didn't spend much time at home either. When we visited his parents, we stayed in his bedroom, and while we did holidays and occasional dinners together, it wasn't like a real family connection.

My dad never really said anything about any of the men I dated. It wasn't until after Don and I divorced that my dad admitted he couldn't stand him from the beginning, but at the time, he kept his opinions to himself.

I wish he had told me what he thought at the start, but I'm not sure I would have listened. There were so many red flags, but because I still hadn't learned to see abusers for what they were, I ignored them all.

Don had a horrible temper from the beginning. He had moments of rage where he would smash car windows, put his hand through the side window, and push me around. Afterward, he would always apologize, saying he didn't mean to do it. I believed I deserved it. He broke my arm while we were dating, but I still married him.

It happened at a bodybuilding contest in Clearwater. I knew a lot of people there and Don was very jealous and got really angry because I was talking to a friend. He left me there, so I ended up arranging a ride home with someone else. Don eventually came back, told me to get in the car, and we drove all the way back to my neighborhood in South St. Pete.

The whole drive was filled with arguing, and he was in a full rage—foaming at the mouth, spitting while he yelled. It was bad. His eyes had this look of complete and utter rage. Any person who has endured this kind of rage from another will understand. There is a look that person has.

Exactly what a predator has when it looks at prey. It's undeniable. I believe it is with all animal species. When we got close to my apartment, which was in a bad area, he pulled over and told me to get out of the car. I refused. He tried to push me out, but I wouldn't budge. He got out of the car, and I locked the doors, including his side so he couldn't pull me out.

That only made him angrier. He banged on the windows, demanding that I get out. He was a big guy—about 5'7" or 5'8" and 245 pounds of solid muscle—so he climbed through the hatch from the back of the car to the front. He grabbed my hair and kept telling me to unlock the door. Eventually, I did.

As soon as he got back into the car, he turned on me and started punching my arm—over and over—until I heard it snap. I was holding my arm, tears in my eyes, and I looked at him and said, "Stop!" He stopped then, but the damage was done. I pulled my hand away, and my bone was clearly broken. It hadn't broken through the skin, but it was close. I told him I needed to go to the hospital.

He was scared he would get arrested, but I promised I wouldn't tell anyone. I said I would tell the hospital staff that I slipped and fell because it was raining. He took me to the hospital, and they questioned me a lot about possible abuse. I stuck to my story, and they put a cast on my arm. It was a compound fracture of the humerus. After that, he calmed down for a little while.

Of course the hospital staff knew. They see abuse cases all the time, and I'm sure they recognized the signs. They had a social worker come in, and both the doctor and nurse asked me about it, but I stuck to my story. I wasn't going to tell them the truth.

And no, it didn't enter my mind to leave. I knew he wasn't a good guy, but I didn't think about leaving. He was on steroids at the time, and he said he was going to stop, which eased his temper a bit, but he still had anger issues. Over time, the hitting became more like pushing—

pushing me into walls or furniture—and there was a lot of verbal abuse. But I honestly believed I deserved it. That's how I was raised—it was all I knew.

I didn't see my dad much during that time, so he didn't know. He may have noticed when I had the cast on my arm, but I told him I'd slipped in the rain, and he didn't press further.

As for my sisters, I didn't have much of a relationship with them. I had no contact with my mom either. It was just me, trying to figure everything out. Alone. My normal.

It was a lot, but I made it through, and it made me stronger. Even in my third marriage, which I'll get to in a bit, there were moments where jealousy and temper flared. Part of me, I think, liked a bit of that challenge. I didn't want to walk all over a man, which I could do, because I'm pretty strong. Like I did with my second husband, my daughters' father. I totally walked all over him.

Finding My Power, Bit by Bit

My second husband never broke my arm or gave me a black eye, but he had his fair share of moments, like pushing me in the heat of an argument. This only happened at the start of our marriage. I was learning. It didn't take long before we established that those behaviors were unacceptable.

Our verbal arguments were fierce. He was clearly a rebound and I was running away from an abusive marriage that I'd got into too early. From the start, this marriage was never going to be loving or functional.

It took years, especially in my third marriage, to figure out what healthy boundaries were and to learn how to fight fair. My third husband, Richard, was the love of my life. He had his flaws; temper, ego-driven, but we are all flawed. He and I did have points early on as well, where he would push and shove, abandon me at a location, and fight unfairly.

When Richard and I started dating, I knew all of his deepest flaws and I accepted them. My boundaries were different then from what they are now, but I'm so glad for our relationship because it enabled me to grow and for us to grow together through the years. We both chose each other. We learned how to work things out and eventually figured out that we just needed space when things got heated—he'd go to one side of the house, and I'd go to the other side of the house. Once we had calmed down, we could come back and talk about it civilly.

On the other hand, my second husband, the father of my kids, was different. He was never jealous, never abusive until the very end of our relationship when things were falling apart. He wasn't smart, and I didn't feel comfortable in that relationship, but it wasn't as toxic as the ones I'd experienced earlier in my life.

That young and early first marriage with Don was difficult. Like my life to that point, it was a period of loneliness, holding onto all the wrong things, and trying to navigate life without the right foundation. But I also know that everything I went through during that time made me stronger.

I was learning about life by watching, listening and jumping all in. At times, holding on too tightly to the wrong things. The wrong people.

A Life Looking for Something Better

As a child and a young adult, every real step forward I took was marked by me setting boundaries, standing up for myself, taking care of myself, and standing strong when those around me would prefer I was weak.

When I look back on my life, it's clear there was nothing I could have done as a kid. I said what I had to say and did what I had to do to protect myself, and even though it was out of character for me, I don't have any regrets.

That moment with my mom, catching her hand, stopped the violence, and in that way, it was necessary. I think my mother felt the weight of my words, even though nothing would have come of them. It wasn't just the words themselves—it was the intensity behind them. She knew, deep down, that I meant it. It must have been visceral for her, too, because she backed off.

It took me a lifetime to get to that point, to stand up for myself in a way I had never done before. I feel incredible blessings and am fortunate that my grandmother, Ruby, stepped in to fill the role of a mother for me as much as she possibly could from Pensacola. She gave me so much of what I needed, and my dad did the best he could, too.

I asked him once, "Why did you leave me in that situation? Why didn't you take me out?" His response was that he had to think of my sisters, too. He couldn't let me dominate the household because, as he said, they would have "gone wild." He said he knew I was strong, that I'd survive. I didn't like being called "his little trooper," but I guess that was his way of justifying things.

We still have different opinions on parenting. I respect his choices, but I've raised my own kids differently. My second greatest accomplishment is that I broke the cycle of abuse. My children have never known the kind of harm I experienced—no physical, emotional, or mental abuse, no addictions. They're thriving, and so am I. It took me longer to get here because I had so much more to unravel, but I finally reached a place of self-love. That's the key—loving yourself. I spent years trying to fill that void with other people or things, but in the end, you have to find that love within yourself. This is my first greatest accomplishment.

Life's storms aren't easy. They're tough, cruel, and brutal. They're painstaking. But the thing is, you can weather the storm—you can make that journey through it to reach the light on the other side. That's what I've come to believe. You have to be strong, determined, and willing to endure. It takes time. You have to be patient with yourself, and forgiving too. I mean really forgiving of yourself!

It's taken me over five decades to get to this point. The point where I know my worth and my value as a human being, and to recognize that the glue holding it all together is self-love.

Getting there wasn't easy. The journey was a storm in itself. We're born perfect, loving people. But the storms of life and the world start layering us with armor, shelling us and shielding that perfection we once had. The real freedom comes when we learn how to release the armor. That's when we can finally be who we truly are.

It's important for people to know that it doesn't come easy. If it did, we'd all be happy. But I know plenty of people who seem to have everything—the money, the looks, the perfect image—and yet, they're still not happy. They don't love themselves. Something inside them keeps holding on to whatever pain or struggle they haven't let go of, and they self-abuse in many different forms.

I know what it's like to be abused, and I know what it's like to self-abuse (eating disorders, abusive marriages, not saying no). It's all part of the journey to get to that place of peace. If I can help someone avoid those landmines—if I can point them out and say, "Maybe don't step there," and empower them to make the right choice, then that's everything. Because it is possible. If it weren't, I wouldn't be standing here today.

That's the heart of it, really. Life is a journey, and it's not all butterflies and sunshine. The tough moments, the struggles—they create the armor we use to protect ourselves. But that same armor also holds us back. Releasing it is what allows us to live freely and to love.

I picture it as breaking away from steel armor, and inside, there's a heart. I think of it visually like that because people always ask, "What would you say to your younger self?" And honestly, I would tell her to stay steadfast. "You can make it through the storm. You can do it. This too shall pass."

It's not about how you go down, it's about how you rise.

We all need a cheerleader, someone who has been through the storm and can say, "I know what those tears of pain feel like." And sometimes that's our grownup selves letting our inner child know it's okay.

There are tears of pain, tears of joy, and neither are weaknesses. Tears are a release. They are strong and a sign of strength. If I can help move you through whatever storm you're facing, then I'll have done something meaningful with this book.

For me, my centered beacon is God. That light first shone for me in my room when I was ten years old, alone and desperate. But I understand that's not everyone's path. People find their light in different ways, and I respect that. What matters is that the light, whether from within or from faith, comes with tenderness, love, and kindness—toward yourself and others.

That's why this book is about one simple truth: You gotta love you. That's the core. Whatever happens, you have to love yourself.

Things will happen in life—hard things, unexpected things—but no matter what, you have to love yourself through it all.

Often in our society, choosing yourself first is considered selfish. I am here to share and change that for you and others.

Selfishness is simply driven by one's ego and what is in their core motives. Choosing yourself first is about being the best person in every way possible. This expands your capability to do more for yourself and others. I shared that my Granddaddy was a Navy Fighter Pilot. Back then they had no oxygen in planes and often, if reaching a certain altitude, the pilot would pass out. This is why, when oxygen masks drop in an airplane, you are told to place the mask on yourself before placing it on others, including children. If you don't follow those instructions, you are likely to pass out and will be unable to help anyone at all. Helping yourself first is in no way selfish. It is smart and selfless. Choose you first!

You perhaps didn't choose yourself first as a child. You didn't know how. Now that you're an adult, you know better. It's okay to do this, not only for yourself but for others in all aspects of your life. Personally, professionally, financially, spiritually, emotionally, mentally. When you Choose You First, you give yourself the wherewithal to help and touch many others in this earthly world.

I've realized that life is a journey, and I'm in a much better place now than I was as that little girl who needed the light of God to shine on her. That light saved me then, and it continues to guide me now. I've learned to break through the armor, and now, I don't take love for granted. I've learned that when you do the work to break free, you gain a whole new appreciation for love and for life itself.

I remember every day, every moment that I get to choose every step made on this continual journey of life.

Falling For My Personal Beliefs

At 22 years old, I was completely focused on being successful in business. I was still with Don (first husband) when I got an opportunity to work for Danka, and I remember talking to my father about it.

"I'm going to be a copier salesman," I said.

To which he said, "That's like the lowest of the low in sales."

"Well," I replied, "then I'll be the best of the low." Then I added, "I'm going to make six figures."

He scoffed while saying my boyfriend and abuser at the time would make six figures before I ever did.

I told him, "Watch me."

From a young age, I've always had this mentality: "Tell me I can't, and I'll prove you wrong."

I dove headfirst into learning the basics of outside sales. While I had a bit of a natural knack for it, I didn't have any formal training. The company, however, had an extensive training program that required making a set number of calls, following scripts, and doing product demonstrations. It was all about repetition and mastering the basics.

I remember being in my studio apartment, practicing my demonstrations on an ironing board as if it were a copier. I practiced until I perfected it.

The job had a lot of accountability. We were supposed to be at work by 8 o'clock, and my manager was strict—if you were even a minute late, she'd lock you out of the meeting. People would bang on the door, but she wouldn't let them in. I never wanted to be that person.

That manager was the same woman who hired me at Danka. She was also an incredible mentor and a great team leader who would give us exercises to improve our skills, which I would practice repeatedly. Sometimes, I stayed at the office until 7 or 9 pm, even though the workday officially ended at five. I was determined to make the most of the materials and training I had, to be the best. Almost certainly, my lack of self-worth drove a need in me to be seen as perfect. So perfect they had to need me and value me. I started to see myself as a "Navy SEAL" of sales, fully committed to excelling.

And it worked. I achieved success in both recognition and income. I was even named Rookie of the Year. It was a large company at the time, and as I stayed on for 14 years, the company continued to grow. My career became the center of my life during that time. Every achievement helped cover up how broken I felt.

Slowly Gaining a Footing in Life

I didn't get married to Don until I was 25, and by then, I'd moved from my studio to a one-bedroom apartment and could afford to buy a decent car on my own.

It was a milestone moment for me. My first car was a Renault Alliance, a car most people haven't heard of because it was only produced for a year. It was a terrible car. By the time I was ready to turn it in, the hood had oxidized so badly that I discovered rubbing vegetable oil on it made it look better. However, in Florida, it rains almost daily. On the day I was driving to trade it in, it started raining, and the oil splashed onto the windshield. My wipers only smeared the oil around, so I had to pull over and wait for the rain to stop. My next car was a 1988 Thunderbird, which I loved. That car felt like a real accomplishment, something I'd earned through my hard work.

That old Renault has always stuck with me as a bit of a life lesson: you can't take anything in life and put a shine on it if it's failing. You have to get to the root of things.

The root of all my problems was one I still hadn't even begun to fix: Myself, my self-worth, and my ability to love myself. It's why, despite the abuse while I was engaged, I still married Don.

Honestly, I thought I was doing okay. Don and I were dating, but we weren't living together. I was out on my own, living independently. I felt a strong sense of pride in what I was building.

At work, we were all women in my office, and we ended up being the top-performing team in the United States one year. It was an empowering experience. The competition was high and we pushed each other forward because we were all working on being the best we could be. They tried putting men in the office, but they didn't last long.

Most people don't stay in the office equipment industry as long as I did, but I enjoyed it and was good at it. My work gave me stability, even when my personal life wasn't steady. After 14 years, I left the company, but before I did, I closed the biggest deal anyone had ever done. I also attended motivational conferences with speakers like Zig Ziglar and Tony Robbins, which kept me motivated and driven.

In hindsight, it wasn't surprising that I was so entirely focused on my work. I was mimicking what I saw my dad do. He escaped into his work and achieved immense success.

Supporting My Husband

When Don and I got married, we were both 25. He was still living with his parents at the time and moved in with me after we tied the knot.

My career flourished from ages 22 to 28, but my marriage did not.

I ended up paying for my husband to go to school and became the decision-maker between us because I was the one earning the money. Still, he liked to feel like he was in charge, I didn't need to push against that—I had my own power through my financial independence.

Again, the signs were there and everyone but me saw it. He was controlling and verbally abusive. Literally, while my maid of honor was walking me down the aisle, she said, "I will turn around with you right now and we will just blow this popsicle stand." I still got married.

Then, once again, a life-changing event took my life over: I was in a snowmobile accident that left me with a traumatic brain injury.

Starting From Scratch

Right after we got married, Don and I went on our honeymoon in Colorado. I'd never seen snow before and we decided to hire snowmobiles. The guide gave us basic instructions, but I lost control of the vehicle, crashed into a tree, and my new husband ran over me, stopping on top of me.

I'd split my head from ear to ear, but with a snowstorm beating down on us, I had to wait for rescue. It took a while, but I was eventually transported to Denver.

I was in critical condition, with paralysis on my right side and a traumatic brain injury. I had to wear a brace and undergo physical and occupational therapy for two years. I had to relearn how to walk, talk, and work. During my recovery, the company I worked for eventually told me I had to return to work. When I did, I found out my manager had given away my entire book of business, so I had to start from scratch, climbing the mountain of success all over again.

Recovery was tough. I struggled with depression and frustration, especially since I had always been a high overachiever in all that I set my mind out to accomplish. Trouble is, that was no longer working for me because my brain needed to heal; it essentially needed the time and therapy to be re-wired.

It was a slow process and I gave myself no grace. My self expectations were demanding. My husband, though supportive in some ways, was busy with his own work and studies. His family helped a lot, but it was still a hard, lonely time for me. I would get so frustrated with my limitations that I started self-harming by hitting myself in the head, which was the only way I knew to release the built-up tension.

Oddly, during that time, anorexia wasn't a major issue for me. In fact, I had gained some weight. I wasn't as big as I would get in later years, but I wasn't anorexic anymore. I can't recall any significant bouts of anorexia after that period. Some of my friends are concerned about my weight now, but it's not like what my anorexia used to look like. I'm at the weight I want to be, and while I wouldn't mind losing more, I definitely don't want to gain any.

As my recovery progressed and I got back to work, I felt like I'd put all my anorexia behind me.

The greatest challenge during those two years of therapy and recovery was the sheer frustration of not being able to do things. My husband wasn't paying much attention, but thankfully, his family stepped in to help. As for my own family, I wasn't connected with them during that period. They knew about my situation, but I don't think they understood how serious it was. It wasn't a big deal to them.

After recovering, I went back to work and had to start over from scratch. But I thought, "If I did it once, I can do it again." And I did.

My Grandmother

During that time, I got a lot of guidance and support from my grandmother. Throughout my life, she was my best friend, a light in my life, the mother I aspired to be. She was so loving and kind, and I can't imagine what I would have done without her influence. We were incredibly close, and I would talk to her every day, even as a teenager and into my twenties.

She was a teacher of life skills. We talked about everything, and although my grandfather, a Navy fighter pilot, was somewhat abusive and very jealous, she had such empathy. When I told her about my husband, Don, and what was going on, she offered support but never encouraged divorce. That wasn't something her generation typically promoted. I valued her advice deeply, and I never wanted to disappoint her.

Every year, she would visit for my birthday on July 2nd. During the last visit before she passed, I remember picking her up from the airport with my dad, and we could see her frailty as she came off the plane. I looked at my dad and said, "It must be hard to see your parent age," and he agreed. It was a moment for both of us, seeing how much she had aged.

It shouldn't have been a surprise. My grandmother had suffered a stroke a few years earlier but had recovered enough to live independently again. She always inspired me with her strength. She'd been through so much, growing up in a large family, and she was such a positive influence on me. Toward the end, we didn't talk as often as we used to, but I felt like she was preparing me for her passing, so I wouldn't be devastated.

Her last visit was in early July 1995. Because of the work my dad did, the Florida Bar

Association Conference had been something we'd attended every year since I was a child. Dad and my stepmother would go earlier than my Grandma Ruby each year as I was older. It gave us our time, and I always enjoyed it. During that visit, she told me she was ready to see my grandfather again and to reunite with her family. It wasn't sad—she said it joyfully as if she was at peace with the idea.

I got a call two days after her return back to her home in Pensacola saying she was in the hospital, and it was serious. I immediately rushed to be with her, and for the next few days, I didn't leave her side. My aunt, uncles and dad encouraged me to take a break, and I reluctantly went to stay at their house. Shortly after, we received another call that she had taken a turn for the worse, and when we arrived at the hospital, the doctor told us she hadn't made it. It was a difficult time, but we held her funeral the next day, and it was attended by so many people who knew her. Her death was on July 13, 1995.

My husband Don came up to be with me after my grandmother passed, but I didn't want him near me. I finally told my dad everything that had been going on in my marriage, and he helped me through the divorce process. My grandmother's passing gave me the clarity to leave. I didn't want to disappoint her, and with her gone, I no longer felt tied to staying in the marriage. I gave Don everything—the house and the material things—and moved to Tennessee to feel safe from potential harm and to start a new life for myself.

Living together for those final weeks was terrible. Don would get enraged, and at times, he even foamed at the mouth like a rabid dog. I knew it was time to go. Interestingly, during my recovery from the snowmobile accident, he never physically abused me—there wasn't really anyone for him to fight with. I was too incapacitated.

Now that I think about it, he had that in common with my mother. They both needed something to fight against to make their abuse seem valid.

When I made the decision to leave Don, I knew my grandmother wouldn't be disappointed in me. I was done with the marriage. I sought support from my dad and his side of the family, not from my sisters. At that time, my sisters were in college. I was completely unattached and disengaged with their lives. I continued to remain disconnected from them while I focused on my own life.

At my grandmother's funeral, I was in such a state of numbness. I was devastated, but it didn't feel real. Oddly, I remember thinking during her last visit to the salon, as we waited to get her chin waxed, "This is what she'll look like when she's gone." It was as if she had prepared me for her passing in so many ways, and yet, when it happened, I felt completely numb. It was a strange, disconnected feeling, like a total emptiness. I think it was a form of self-preservation because she had been my emotional rock.

Looking back on that seven-year period of my life, from 22 to 28, I was so young and naive. I felt invincible, and that feeling of invincibility acted like a kind of armor for me, especially when facing adversity. The snowmobile accident and my grandmother's death made that armor even stronger. It allowed me to stand up for myself, even when it came to divorcing my abuser. I learned that it was okay to say no and to handle rejection, both in my personal life and in my career. I became more resilient. At the time, I didn't understand that the thing I was really looking for was acceptance. More than that, self-acceptance, peace, and the ability to see my vulnerability as a strength.

None of that was on my radar. It was about being a Rambo—about what I could do to push through the trenches of life. Whatever life threw at me, I was going to get through it.

And honestly, that mentality served its purpose, but it all came at a price. I wasn't authentic. I wasn't kind. I was driven and egotistical. I was a professional primadonna with no real emotional connections. Looking back on those years, I can see all the things I learned, and also all the mistakes I made. I remember thinking how I didn't like the person in the mirror.

I said I felt blank when my grandmother passed. In a way, that ability to disconnect was like a survival tool. I've never been in the military, but I can imagine that kind of detachment is something like what they experience. Being a "sales SEAL" was about training myself to separate my emotions and mental self from my physical self. That's how I started out in life, and I carried that skill into my twenties, using it to navigate the challenges thrown at me. I still do it now and then, if I experience physical or emotional pain. The difference is that now I am conscious and fully aware of doing it.

This disconnect certainly helped lead me through difficult times, so much so that I wasn't even aware of the emotional cost. Little did I know, different kinds of emotions were going to ramp up pretty soon!

My father expedited my divorce from my first husband within 30 days of my filing. Since I wanted nothing but out, there wasn't a lot to discuss. Getting out was the only thing I wanted.

Just fifteen days after my divorce was finalized, I was in Rochester, New York, attending a two-week-long training session with a group of sales professionals. As you can imagine, not a lot happens in Rochester. But for me, it was the start of a new phase. It's where I met my second husband.

New Explorations

Age 28. What a time! I don't even know where to begin. Looking back, that was a pivotal year. I'd lost my grandmother and had mustered the courage to say "I'm out" of an abusive marriage.

I was free. I walked away from everything and threw myself into work. That became my escape, and I thought I was thriving. Financially, I was doing great, and I felt empowered—not real empowerment, as I understand it today, but more of a work-driven obsession. I became a workaholic.

Two weeks after the divorce, I attended a training meeting in Rochester, New York, during winter. Rochester is all snow, snow, snow in the winter, so we were stuck indoors for two weeks. Naturally, you get close to your teammates during training, and these were people from all over the country. We went to dinners, had drinks, and bonded. For the first time in my adult life, I wasn't attached to anyone. I remember feeling a sense of freedom.

There were a couple of guys there I found attractive, and one of them showed a lot of interest in me. At first, I thought we were just having fun, but by the end of the training, he was in tears. He didn't want to leave. He was married, and he didn't want to go home. I was in shock. I told him he had to go back to his wife. But even after we went home, he kept calling and pursuing me. Eventually, we developed a friendship that turned into more.

It was a complete rebound. Weeks after my divorce, and there I was, meeting him in Tennessee. He filed for divorce, and we both transferred within our company to Knoxville.

Suddenly, we were living together, working together, and planning a life. It all moved so fast, and before I knew it, we were getting married. My dad and stepmom were concerned—they'd never seen married people fight like we did, even on our wedding day.

A Seed Is Planted

With all this happening so fast, I do need to add one small but critical moment. Before Chris (second husband) and I got married, we were living together in Knoxville. During that time, I joined a country club as a charter member, and Richard Bishop joined at the same time.

Richard Bishop. Remember that name.

One day, I happened to bump into Richard coming out of the ladies' bathroom. When our eyes met, it was magic. He said, "Hello, I'm Richard Bishop, and you are?"

We shared a lot of social time within our circle of friends and were never short of conversation and fun together.

He was married and I was getting married. At the time, we called it mutual admiration. Neither of us acted on it. But later, we admitted that it was love at first sight.

By the time Chris and I got married, Richard and I had been orbiting each other's lives for a year. At the time, I had no idea the role Richard would play in my life. None at all.

Back To My Second Husband

Like my first husband, I married someone who was determined to keep me small. Our relationship had a lot of arguments, many fueled by drinking. He resented my success in the office. I was outshining him, and the management loved me, which only deepened his insecurities. He felt small and insignificant, while I felt he wasn't adequate. We had fundamental differences. He constantly played the victim, and it wore me down.

I stayed on the train just like my dad did in our family. I put on my masks at each turn and thought I was masterful in my performance. I was out to prove to everyone what a big shot I was with all that I had gained. But a performance for no one is not a performance. Often not even very good.

Chris and I bought a house and built a social life. Again, I was the one paying for everything, but he was happy to enjoy the perks and act like he was the one providing it all.

In retrospect, I was just living my own lie. Trying to pretend I had everything but actually, I had nothing. My marriage was empty, but I did nothing to change it.

Even though I'd locked eyes on Richard, and had that amazing connection, I still married Chris. A man I had no respect for. What made me think I could make that marriage into the perfect fairytale ending?

Love At First Sight

We had our first child, Lexi, when I was 32. I had always wanted to be a mom, and from the moment she was born, I was completely in love. Everything about her was perfect. I couldn't get enough of her, kissing her, holding her—she was everything I had ever dreamed of. The birth was easy, and planned, with an epidural. I took 90 days off, using all my accrued vacation time, and honestly, I didn't want to go back to work. But financially, I had to because my new husband wasn't making much money at the time. He had left our company and started selling insurance, but he struggled, and I began to accept what I had gotten myself into. This wasn't the white-picket-fence life I had imagined. Once again, I was supporting my husband.

Our relationship was full of conflict. His family never accepted me, likely because he had left his first wife for me. I felt isolated, entertaining his family while hiding in the kitchen during gatherings. Financially, I was the one carrying the burden, but they blamed me for his overspending. It was incredibly frustrating.

I would drop Lexi off at daycare and throw myself back into work. I convinced myself that I had it easier than stay-at-home moms because at least I could use my brain and have adult conversations. But looking back, I know that I wasn't being authentic. I was hiding behind work, wearing a mask, pretending to be everything I thought people expected me to be—successful, in control, the perfect mom, wife, and professional - everything my mother wasn't. I wasn't ready to be selfless in a relationship, and I kept letting life's wheels turn without stopping to ask myself, "What am I really doing?"

When I was 35, we had our second child, Brittany. I was hesitant at first because I loved Lexi so much and didn't know if I could love another child the same way. But we got pregnant quickly. My second pregnancy was difficult. At 20 weeks, I went into preterm labor. I didn't even recognize it for what it was at first. I was still working, still trying to juggle everything. My husband wasn't very supportive—he didn't even come to the hospital when I went into labor early. I had to go through it alone, but that was what I was used to in my life.

Brittany was a challenging baby. She was colicky and difficult, the complete opposite of Lexi. We ended up hiring an au pair to help, but it wasn't a good solution. It just deferred my responsibilities as a mother, and I wasn't as connected to Brittany as I was to Lexi.

At that time, I had been forced back into the role of the working executive and making money so we could afford our lifestyle. I say forced, but my career had taken an upward trajectory. I began in little Knoxville Tennessee and was now working on a deal on office equipment that would encompass all the United States, Canada and Mexico. As an accomplishment, it was beyond exhilarating. From the inception of the Request for Proposal to the Terms and Conditions Negotiations that included cross-border legalities.

Our office equipment dealership was struggling. The stock tanked, and we had gone through four CEO changes during this process. I was awarded the contract for my company over other international and national manufacturers and dealerships. Nothing was going to stop me.

Around that time, we upgraded our house and moved to a more affluent neighborhood. I was juggling everything—work, building the house, and two young children. It was overwhelming, but I kept pushing through. Business as usual.

Chris and I continued to have a tumultuous relationship. He resented my success, and I resented his lack of it. He started going to strip clubs, spending money we didn't have, and we fought constantly. Then, when Brittany was two, my mother died.

A Weight Is Lifted

I had no real relationship with my mother at that point—she had held Lexi once as a baby, but I had distanced myself for my children's sake.

I went to her funeral alone, not to grieve but to support my sisters. I felt no sadness, only relief that she was finally free from her demons—mental illness, alcoholism, and the destructive patterns she lived by. My role as the oldest sibling took over, and I did what needed to be done, I was emotionally disconnected. It was mechanical, like everything else in my life at that point. I was a shell of who I once was, hiding behind the different masks I wore—mother, wife, daughter, and professional.

A Chance Meeting

Chris stayed at home with the girls while I was at the funeral. When I came back, I brought my aunt Paula (my mother's step-sister) and her daughter, her husband, and their child, hoping to rekindle a relationship with them. I thought, "It's fall, and it's beautiful here!" The fall leaves were gorgeous, and even though it was a busy time, I wanted to show them around.

They stayed at our house, and we decided to visit Cades Cove, which is a big natural loop with restored old churches and abundant wildlife—deer, bears, everything. It was a fabulous trip. Chris chose to play golf instead of joining us and I didn't mind. We were utterly disengaged and I didn't want him around.

We had all the little ones—my two girls and their child—so we took two separate cars because of the car seats. At some point during the trip, our car broke down. We were in the very back of the park, miles into the loop, and it was getting dark. The little shops were closing, and we were completely stranded with no cell service.

The kids were crying—they were hungry—and it was pitch black. There were no lights, and no one was around. We managed to get a park ranger to call a tow truck, but it felt like it took forever. As we waited in the dark, we saw headlights coming down the path, and at first, we thought it was a motorcycle gang coming to rob us in the woods! We were freaking out, locking the car doors, and trying to figure out how to protect the kids. But as they got closer, we realized It was just a group of cyclists, out for an evening ride. Crazy thoughts go through your head when you are alone in the back of the dark woods thinking you must protect your babies.

Like I was going to spin around and become a superhero to protect us all? We were so relieved!

Eventually, the tow truck arrived, and we got out of there, heading into Gatlinburg to grab some food after our exhausting ordeal. By the time I got cell service again, Chris was furious that he hadn't been able to reach me. So we agreed to meet at a restaurant in Pigeon Forge called Connor's to eat before we headed for home.

The restaurant was packed—it's always busy in the fall. Chris was at the bar holding Lexi, and I had Brittany in my arms. Then, while we were waiting for our food, out of the blue, who should walk up but Richard Bishop.

Once again, the attraction was instant and intense. I was love-struck the day I first saw him, and nothing had changed.

Richard had recognized Chris at the bar, even with the crowds of people around. He had his youngest daughter with him and went over to chat, making small talk about how they were building a cabin and gathering supplies.

Then Richard asked, "Where's Michelle?" Chris pointed over to where I was sitting with Brittany, and Richard came over to say hello.

It was the first time we'd seen each other in over seven years, and instantly, I felt the same spark I had all those years ago. The same electricity. We talked briefly, caught up on life, and he mentioned that he now had a life insurance brokerage firm. Since I was also in insurance at the time, we talked about how we could collaborate.

We exchanged numbers, and eventually, we scheduled a business meeting. He came to my office, and we talked for hours about life, family, and business. The conversation flowed so easily, and there was such great energy between us. It had been the same way all those many years ago.

As he was leaving, I gave him a hug—I'm a hugger—but this hug felt different. There was an unmistakable connection. It wasn't just a casual hug; there was something more. I had never experienced a feeling like that ever in my entire life.

I was existing in a loveless marriage, supporting and growing a family in a big house. I drove a Mercedes, was a member of country clubs, had social connections, and ran my own business, yet I was empty inside. It was all a lie from the beginning; a lie I had been feeding myself my whole entire life.

Richard and I scheduled another lunch to talk further about business, but when the day came, he didn't show up. I was furious. Nobody had ever no-showed on me before, especially for something as important as business. I called his office, and after being put on hold for way too long, someone told me that Richard Bishop had "left the building." I was livid.

I left a voicemail, saying, "Richard Bishop, this is Michelle Eineke. We had a lunch appointment, and you no-showed. You are the hottest and coldest man I have ever met in my life!" I hung up in frustration and immediately regretted it. I replayed the message in my head, realizing how it might come across—way more charged than I intended.

The next day, he called to apologize. He explained that he had gotten sick after an outing with his daughter, which was very rare for him, and he asked if we could reschedule. We agreed to meet at a small pub, OCI (Old College Inn). It was dark, quiet, and we didn't know anyone there. As soon as we sat down, I told him, "I can't do this." He asked what I meant, and I explained, "I want you to know the real me, not just the business me or the friend me. The real me." The feelings were mutual.

At that point, we were both still married, but I knew my marriage was over. I got an attorney, found the best representation I could, and filed for divorce in early December. After my mom passed in October, I felt like I had permission to finally end this marriage. I was exhausted from carrying all the weight and pretending to be someone I wasn't. I was tired of the masks. It was time.

New Beginnings

Chris was served with divorce papers right between the eyes when he returned from a trip to visit his family. He was upset, but I didn't care. I told my attorney I didn't want to fight over anything—I was willing to walk away. My lawyer warned me that this wouldn't be easy, but I knew I could handle it. Chris signed the papers, and I agreed to joint custody of the kids, which, in hindsight, I would never do again. Lexi and Brittany were only two and four at the time.

Richard and I had already developed a deeper connection by then. We shared a kiss in the car the night he told me he was "all in," even though he made it clear that he wouldn't leave his marriage until his oldest daughter graduated from high school. I accepted that because I loved him. I think, deep down, I'd loved him since the moment we met.

By the beginning of February 2004, my divorce was finalized and I was willing to wait for Richard. But his wife had found out about us when Chris's sister wrote a note and left it in Richard's mailbox, exposing our affair.

Richard's wife didn't confront him about it; she just filed for divorce without asking him anything.

Richard had been in a miserable marriage for years, and this wasn't the first time they'd had marital issues. She filed at the beginning of February 2004 and served him the papers the day my divorce was complete and final. Despite Richard's divorce taking three and a half years to be finalized, the property division would take many years more.

Finally, The Right Man

Richard and I got married in January 2007, just weeks after his divorce was finalized. I was 41 by then and was excited to be his wife and be able to begin our life together. The battle to get to this point had taken such a toll on me and him. I remember the moment his divorce was final, we walked out of the courthouse with his attorney and we had to stop for a minute because my body was physically shaking. Was it finally over?

I was sad about it, not happy. I'm not a selfish person. This whole thing had taken so much away from every one of us. His ex-wife, me, him, the children. It's a piece of yourself in those moments that are forever lost. I felt relief and exhaustion, but it still wasn't over. It would be another six years before all the legal battles finally ended.

From beginning to end, Richard's wife did everything she could to make things as difficult as possible. She'd kicked him out as soon as she found out about the affair, changed the locks, and completely ambushed him. She alienated him from both of his kids and spun her own version of the truth. She even filed an injunction against me and told their children her version of the story. When she filed for divorce, she told Richard's sister that she was going to take the shirt off his back. In the end, she didn't just take the shirt—he had less than nothing when we got married. He went from having a comfortable life to having no life at all financially. Once again, I found myself back in the role of supporting a man, but this was different. He was different. He was smart, strong and had an incredible zest for life and success.

This process emasculated him. Because he carried himself with such confidence and acted like an alpha male who had everything under control, people assumed he still had money, but it wasn't true. He had nothing. Still, I was okay being the silent partner because I loved him unconditionally. I knew what he was capable of as a leader and a partner. I knew this was just a challenge for us to overcome. Above all, I knew what he could create with my support. Support he had never really received before, not as a boy, a young man and even a grown adult with all his knowledge and years of experience.

Working together to build our lives up from nothing was exciting, fun, challenging, and ultimately, an incredible accomplishment.

Unlike my previous husbands, Richard was hard-working, charismatic, and had an innate ability to lead. Such a strength. After we got through the chaos of legal challenges and distraction from his divorce, he focused on business and financial recovery.

Together, we were a force to be reckoned with. Our ability to rise to the challenge of life yielded an extremely successful career in the life insurance industry. He liked to work hard and play hard. Larger than life, he went from not making any money for years due to the shackles put on him by his divorce to earning in abundance.

Our lifestyle was truly amazing. Richard was very giving to me as his wife. We shopped at Gucci, Louis Vuitton, Cartier, and Tiffany to name only a few. We'd go from Rodeo Drive in California to 5th Avenue in NY. We had an almost 6,000-square-foot home that we had completely remodeled. Seven cars, an antique classic 442 car, 4 off-road vehicles, a couple of jet skis, a pontoon boat and a yacht. He loved hunting. We had a gun collection of over 60 guns.

It seemed wherever we traveled, he wanted to buy a home there. At one point we owned 14 properties. We did a lot of traveling and always went first class. Richard and I traveled not just in the United States but abroad. We would always stay at the best hotels; Four Seasons but typically Ritz Carlton. Suites and Concierge Level always. In the years leading to his death, we would travel to Laguna Nigel, CA at least twice a year, Florida several times, and then an annual trip to Monterrey, California to stay in Pebble Beach. Our travels incorporated business and pleasure. We traveled to Kentucky, Maine, Arkansas, Arizona, New York, Montana, Illinois, Louisiana, Georgia, North Carolina, South Carolina, Mississippi, Arkansas, Texas, Virginia, Kentucky, Washington D.C., Nevada, Colorado, Wyoming, Kansas, Minnesota, Washington, Alaska, Hawaii. He took me to Ireland twice, Prague, Paris, Venice, Amsterdam, Holland, and Bora Bora.

The problem is that he was an all-or-nothing type of man and he took big risks. His financial web was extremely tangled. Fortunately, I was looped into every aspect of it. We never kept anything from each other. Now that doesn't mean he listened to me! There were risks and decisions he made that I disagreed with. We always came to a mutual decision in the end. It was a true partnership.

The biggest error, however, was that neither of us had a will. We just figured he would live forever. We always said we'd get an attorney to draw up our wills, but we just never got around to it. The consequence was that there was a lot to untangle at his death.

My children were not included in consideration of our assets that we worked so hard together to build, nor were they wholly recognized in their grief. He was their father figure since they were two and four years of age. His influence was so impactful to them. This is not to diminish the loss of him to his own biological children. The death of him impacted our whole families, friends and business associates.

The complications after Richard's death weren't helped by the turmoil we experienced with their mother and her inability to co-parent and have a civil relationship. He loved all his girls. Together, we were a blended family.

The divorce had left so many scars. The property settlement had dragged on for years. Even after the divorce was finalized, it went to judgment, which was then appealed. The case was sent to a special master, who upheld the original judgment, but it was appealed again to the State Supreme Court. It wasn't until around 2013 that everything was finally settled—six years after the divorce itself. The case involved hundreds of thousands of dollars, expert witnesses, appraisals, and countless delays. Even after that, they went after child support, back child support, and anything else they could.

The situation was nothing less than difficult on every member of the family. His ex-wife was hurt and damaged by years of the relationship with Richard - going back to high school. A lot of pain comes from growing up with someone through the years. We are all flawed. She was and remains to be a devoted mother to her children.

The tentacles of hurt that spread as a result of the selfish actions Richard and I took in our love for each other touched everyone in each of our families. Boundaries of yesterday, life consequences, lessons learned, and the decisions that mold us into the people we are today - every day we wake and get to choose how we live.

Blended Families

During this time, Richard's youngest daughter, Lillian, went through a rebellious phase and wasn't doing well at school. Not unusual. She was a teenager. All teenagers go through this phase. Some more than others.

Her mother, who maintained primary custody of their youngest, allowed us limited time with her, but we always made the most of it.

Then Lillian got involved with a 27-year-old man, 10 years older than her. Richard was heavily involved with a non-profit at the time, and this man was connected to the organization. Lillian's mother found out and showed up at my house, which she had never done before. Everything exploded.

I sat down with his daughter, her mom, and Richard and told them that this had to stop! I suggested that both his daughter and the ex-wife move in with us so we could all live under one roof and focus on being a family. I moved them out of their apartment, cared for them, bought Lillian's mother new clothes, and did everything I could to help her. We ate together, we worshipped together, we traveled together, we did a lot of talking together. It was a time of healing to whatever degree would be allowed by all.

Richard was often away during this time because it was hunting season, so I was the one handling everything—his ex-wife, daughter, and all the logistics. Things were never really good between Richard and his ex.

For the sake of the children, I truly tried to build a relationship with his ex-wife, and it worked for a while. We did, however, have some strange moments—like her sitting at the edge of our bed in the morning while Richard and I were still in pajamas, drinking coffee and chatting.

She and I would stay up to all hours of the morning talking. I had to travel for work and oddly enough, I would feel comfortable with her in my home with my husband alone.

My intention was only to heal our relationships and make things better for everyone. During this time, a trust was built to the extent that as a collective group there was a final agreed settlement regarding financial matters pending in the courts that was resolved in the best interest of not only her but everyone emotionally. Through all our conversations I got to really understand her bitterness, and most importantly, I was able to apologize from my soul for the hurt that had been caused, with the intent to place her in a better position than she ever would be if we had not gathered together.

I will always be grateful for this time of openness and forgiveness on both our parts.

Good Things Don't Always Last

However, after a few months, things started to unravel. It got to a point when I had to tell Richard it was time for her to move out.

I started to get an uncomfortable sense that she was becoming bitter about the life that Richard and I had built and that she was feeling entitled to what we had worked so hard to fight back from. There was no way I was going to backstroke on the progress made within the family. I told Richard, it was time for her and their daughter to move.

I worked with a realtor and found a perfect home for her and their daughter —close to school and work, and in a good price range. Richard and I paid a large down payment to make sure she could afford the monthly mortgage. We also covered all moving and storage costs from her apartment, utility start-up costs, etc. I wanted her to have a good life, and I genuinely wanted peace within our family. Just as I predicted, when she eventually sold that house, she made a far greater profit than expected based on the numbers at that time. She made the decision to move closer to her oldest daughter and I wish her the life that she aspires to have for herself.

The Fixer

When Richard and I committed to marriage in 2007, I was all in—biblically, emotionally, everything. It was us against the world. I tirelessly made sure I had Richard's back, even when he faltered, which he did at times. He played big and hard. That's just the kind of man he was. When he burned bridges, I went back and mended them. That's what I did in our relationship. Truth is, he wouldn't just burn a bridge; he'd burn it, explode it, and then run over it again.

I was the fixer in our relationship. It was my role. Even with his ex and Lillian, I knew what I was getting into when I invited them into our home. They never had a good relationship, so this was going to be up to me as a miracle worker to figure out. He was always upfront with me on it. Again, my boundaries were different then than they are now. I loved him and knew exactly what I was getting into with him. I have no regrets even though anyone else would most likely not have accepted such terms.

We were happy and in love, and we argued! These arguments mostly stemmed from Richard's jealousy, insecurities, and mistrust. He was often jealous of other men, accusing me of looking for attention, which made me withdraw. I let him take the role of the dad, and I wanted him to be that strong figure for my kids. They needed that, and I wanted to model what I thought a wife should be.

Richard was a big drinker. He was high-functioning, never missing work or obligations, but as he got older, his drinking became sloppy. I never tried to set parameters for him; instead, I tried to control the environment—like making sure he was in a safe place when he drank too much. People noticed his controlling behavior toward me, like the time he told me I couldn't wear a pair of leopard heels I loved because he didn't like them. I complied without even thinking about it.

As our relationship progressed, I gained weight—about 70 pounds—while he stayed in great shape. I didn't want to gain weight, it's just something that happened over time. Richard preferred me heavier as it inhibited my confidence. The fact that he never struggled with his weight made me more self-conscious. He was a lady's man, that's for sure. He loved the pretty women, and they loved him. It was a difficult balancing act. When I made a move towards losing weight it would create conflict with him asking why I was doing it. I simply stopped trying to lose it because I didn't want it to be an issue. I was always received well by others regardless of my weight, but it wasn't something I was happy about. It created huge insecurities in me. I tried to be what he wanted, but I wasn't being authentic in my personal appearance.

Noticing The Pattern

I've come to realize that every one of my husbands shared a common trait: they all wanted me to be professionally, emotionally, and spiritually smaller than I was capable of being. They all tried to suppress my spirit, and that stems from my relationship with my dad. I've recently done deep work through therapy, which has helped me uncover these patterns. For so long, I believed I wasn't good enough, pretty enough, or quiet enough. I was taught to be seen and not heard, and that left me feeling small, even though I have a big personality.

I'm still working on this, learning to quiet the voices that hold me back and to live authentically.

It's a journey, not something that can be fixed in a few days of therapy. I'm still growing, and I'm excited about the progress I'm making. It's about finding love within myself and living from a place of love, not just the power of it.

I'm shifting and changing, and I won't let anything or anyone hold me back anymore. I'm growing, and I'm living full and large, continuing to practice what I've learned.

Writing this book is part of that process. It's helping me open some of the volumes in that library in my head that I thought I'd closed forever.

Almost everything I did during this period, I chose to do. Much of it was necessary, but I got to choose. We always have a choice, and I'm more aware of that now.

Chaos and Passion

The start of my relationship with Richard was so easy. I had made a full commitment to him. I wasn't putting on any pretense. I was completely transparent, and we had fun. We never, even up to the day he passed, had a moment in our entire relationship where we didn't talk about anything and everything. That was amazing to me. That two people would be so at ease with each other despite the turmoil of the divorce and family life.

Besides thinking he was incredibly handsome, charismatic, and smart, I liked a good challenge. I'm a smart person, and I didn't want a man who wasn't up to that. More than that, I needed to trust him. When you take off the armor you've built over the years, it leaves you very vulnerable, and I trusted him to take care of me in that vulnerability. He was always protective, which I respected and appreciated. I loved his intelligence, strength, and the passion he had for everything he did. He was so kind to everyone. People thought he was their best friend. He remembered little things like calling people to ask, "Isn't your son graduating?" He was that way with everyone, no matter their social or economic background, and I felt honored that he chose me to share his life with.

We traveled a lot, and I explored things outside of my comfort zone. My idea of getting meat was going to the grocery store and picking up whatever the butcher had, but he exposed me to hunting.

I had never held a gun in my life. It wasn't something I would have normally done, but I wanted to spend time with him. There were some amazing sunsets and sunrises, the sound of nature, and the whole idea of hunting was fascinating to me. He wanted to teach me, and he always emphasized safety first. I liked to joke that I was a "glam hunter" because he took care of everything. He made sure I was in the right spot and wearing the right gear. When we did hunt, he would retrieve it, but I helped clean it out and cook it, and learned a lot from the experience.

One time, while driving down the highway, I asked, "What is that?" and he said, "Honey, they call that cotton." I was amazed. My idea of cotton was cotton balls from the drugstore, but seeing it growing in fields was a completely new experience. He pulled over, and I picked some. That wonderment was exhilarating. We had some funny times and some not-so-funny times, but they were all great experiences.

Nothing was ever dangerous, but things like duck hunting and sitting in blinds with frogs and other creatures were interesting. I've always been a girly girl, so I had to adjust. But I learned to appreciate the ecosystem and the fact that we ate what we hunted, rather than just hunting for trophies. I learned about overpopulation and how it can lead to disease, which made me respect the process more.

It was all about constant learning for me. We traveled to places like Pebble Beach, the Swiss Alps, and France. We stayed in everything from fine hotels to tents. We experienced everything from one end of the spectrum to the other, which made our relationship wondrous. But it wasn't perfect. He could be incredibly sharp-tongued and had the ability to burn down a bridge with his words. He always went big, whether it was good or bad. If he wasn't happy, you knew it. At that stage of my growth, I accepted his jealousy and his traditional views about gender roles. My boundaries and understanding of those roles have changed since, but in that time, our marriage worked.

Another Twist of Fate

It was the end of 2015. I was getting ready to turn 50. I thought okay, I guess I better have a mammogram. The results of this diagnostic test were something that would put me and our whole family in a life-altering spiral. The test revealed a mass, and after the biopsy, it was determined that I had breast cancer.

Things were finally good. I had a successful career selling medical equipment that I'd built up over the last 10 years, my marriage was solid, we didn't have any family legal turmoil going on, and we were traveling, boating, and enjoying friends. But suddenly our relationship and the whole world as I knew it was going to change.

When I got the diagnosis, I pulled out my trusty tool: physical and mental dissociation. With the knowledge I'd gained in my work, I went into the whole process, from treatment to recovery, like a clinician.

Underneath the surface though, there was always this underlying concern for me emotionally: would I lose Richard?

Richard was a "leg man," and I was this five-foot girl. Clearly not the kind of woman he usually went for. One time, in the kindest and funniest way, I was running on the beach towards Richard, and he burst out in laughter. Here I'm thinking this is a Bo Derek moment. I said, "What in the world are you laughing so hysterically about?" He said, "Honey you are so cute, you look like a penguin running under the moonlight."

When I got a cancer diagnosis, I was convinced that he would abandon me like everyone that I cared about always did in my past. As I shared this deepest darkest concern with my Aunt, she said very simply, "Michelle, you are not giving him enough credit."

From the beginning, Richard never missed a single appointment. He was my support and cheerleader without judgment. He was a good man and my Aunt was right. I hadn't given him enough credit. His love and support never wavered.

Family Ties

I'm glad I allowed myself to be vulnerable, even though it led to emotional disruptions in our relationship. We faced difficulties, especially because of our previous marriages, but I never wanted to be anything but his wife first and foremost, and I always respected his two children. I recognized that they had a mother, but I was their cheerleader and cared for them as I would my own children. His daughters never had issues with my girls.

Richard's oldest had graduated from high school around the time of the divorce, so she was very angry with him. He loved her deeply, and her rejection destroyed him. They did develop some sort of relationship later, but it was never on firm ground. Even now, after his passing, I had hoped we could all come together as a family, but that chapter closed with his death. His daughters moved on, and they have their own lives, heavily influenced by their mother's perspective I suspect. I've accepted that I don't have a relationship with them, and I'm okay with that.

For the longest time, I fought for a relationship with them. I reached out and wanted so much to connect. I knew I couldn't have a relationship with their mother, but I didn't think that would prevent me from having one with them.

His oldest is now in her mid-thirties with two children. Her mother lives close by and helps care for them. They have their own lives, and I respect that. I want nothing but health, happiness, and joy for them. I understand they probably believe they weren't treated fairly after their father's death, but they received their share fairly according to the law.

Their father passing without a will caused a whole lot of issues, especially since the relationships with his daughters remained fragile even up to his death. If a will had been drafted, as strong-headed as he was, it is likely that nothing would have been dispersed financially. He would likely have fought the court system as hard as he had during the divorce. He'd have created a will that meant his estate would have come to me and no one else. On one hand, contribution and emotional support for others were important to him, but it was often filled with righteousness and judgment.

I view these events very differently because of my life thread. I see the sadness, pain, loss. He loved his girls with all of his being regardless of anything they did or said. In fact, when we first got together we made a joint commitment: our children would always be loved by each other as if our blood runs through them.

Our love was so great for each other that the choice was to love with joy each and every child. It was beautiful and real. So, when I heard that the youngest even said on video that I was a "gold-digging slut" who took all their father's money and left them with nothing, it hurt.

His youngest child was more integrated into our family unit. As a supporter through most of her life, that was shocking to hear, but I suspect her mother fueled that perception. It was hurtful, but I've come to terms with it.

Since Richard's death, I have never asked to be present in the pregnancies, births, or lives of either of his oldest daughters' children, or his youngest daughter's wedding or any major life events.

I don't regret the decisions I made. I fulfilled my responsibilities and did my best. You can't control how people perceive things, but you can control how you choose to move forward.

Acceptance

For a long time, I wanted everyone to get along and be at peace, but now I know that's not always possible. I did everything I could, and if it wasn't enough for some people, that's something I've learned to live with. I'm okay with how things turned out, and I'm okay with how they feel. I've accepted that they are living their lives, just not with me, and that's not necessarily a bad thing. Life moves forward, and we make choices that shape our paths.

I am so fortunate that there is a loving part of his family who still includes me in everything. It means so much to me. He had a huge family of aunts, uncles, cousins, nephews, nieces, and most of all his sisters and their husbands. Unfortunately, his youngest sister unexpectedly passed not too long after he did, but his oldest sister Donna and her husband Bob are still great friends and the closest ties I have to his family. I will be forever grateful for the support of the Bishop family in accepting me and not abandoning me on the death of such a significant man as Richard.

I Choose Me

In the years since his passing, I've worked on myself, and I've grown stronger. I choose me now. I realize that I deserve to love myself and to be my own advocate. I need to have a voice, and there's nothing wrong with that. I'm learning to be kind, vulnerable, and accepting of what people bring to the table. What they bring is their story, it's not mine. I've learned to stop telling myself negative stories, the ones filled with fear from so long ago, hiding in the shadows, trying not to disrupt anything. Now, I'm shedding that armor, bit by bit.

It's a process. The armor gets thinner and lighter every day. I still have dents like the Tin Man, but I'm moving forward.

I deserve to make choices for myself, to live lighter, and to breathe in life. In every way, I'm letting go of what doesn't serve me.

It took me a long time, but I've learned that putting myself first isn't taking anything away from others; it's actually giving my true self, vulnerable and open, to whatever may come. There will always be obstacles, but I don't let them stop me.

I've also come to understand that being authentic and honest with myself is what matters most. Whether it's in relationships, work, or just day-to-day life, I have to honor my own integrity. For example, when I was younger, I would show up two hours late to meet friends, and they would just accept it. Now, I recognize how disrespectful that was, not only to them but to myself. It's all about honoring commitments, even the ones only you know about.

This realization has been a huge awakening for me, and I'm learning every day. It's a daily process, and I still slip up. But I know now that it's about being conscious of what I say, how I act, and how I treat myself and others. If we could all live with more consciousness and awareness, what a different world it would be.

Discovering Who I Really Am

My Greatest Loss

I am 58 at the time of writing. Richard passed away when he was 60, and I was 53. Of all the losses in my life, losing Richard hit me most.

His date of death was August 8, 2019. I traveled with him frequently, just not this week. For years after his passing, I blamed myself for not being there. If I had, this would have never happened. I always took care of him. But this time, I wasn't there, and the tragedy of his loss will ripple through the rest of my life.

Richard had been really running and gunning it all week. He had traveled by plane and car, going from our place in Tennessee down to Georgia, then flying across the United States to Minnesota. He was there for a huge presentation with some brokers, introducing them to the wholesale division of a company (we can't use any names). He was supposed to come home on a Friday morning flight. He arrived there on the Wednesday before, and I talked to him throughout the day—first thing on Thursday morning and again in the evening before they went on their river cruise.

One of his colleagues had a yacht, and the evening entailed taking a group of six agents, brokers, and financial planners out to dinner, followed by a cruise down the Mississippi River to see the Twin Cities, St. Paul and Minneapolis, at sunset. They did that cruise and came back. Richard stayed on the boat with his colleague, as it had two bedrooms, while others returned to the hotel.

From what I understand (since I wasn't there), as the group was walking down the dock to the van, they heard a splash from the bow of the boat, which was still in dock. They only heard one splash and no other sounds, but they immediately thought of Richard. They ran back to the boat, and Richard wasn't on the bow. One of the men jumped into the water, while another person with a boat nearby tried to help, while they called 911.

The captain, Richard's colleague, shone a light in the water, but they couldn't find him. The water was only seven to eight feet deep, and Richard was a six-foot-tall man. He didn't struggle. He didn't try to surface for air.

During the autopsy, they found that he had no broken bones, no stroke, no heart attack—nothing was physically wrong. The only mark on him was a small scratch on the left side of his lip. He'd drowned.

I've heard that in fresh water it can take as little as 30 seconds to lose consciousness and drown. Even so, the idea that he never struggled or splashed?

We had experience with boats; we owned a yacht, a pontoon, and two ski boats. Richard was a great swimmer and water skier, so it wasn't due to inexperience. The only factors they could point to were the trip hazards on the boat, which he wasn't familiar with, and his blood alcohol level, which was high. He had been entertaining all week, so that was the reality of the situation. His blood alcohol was very high, and I think, ultimately, he just lost his equilibrium. It was late, around 10 p.m., and I believe he went to the bow, maybe to relieve himself, and fell in. He was inebriated, lost his balance, and couldn't recover. When I saw his body later, his fingernails had dirt under them, which he never had. I think he tried to grab onto something but couldn't make it back up.

Alcohol and boating are a dangerous combination. Richard had been working and entertaining all week, and I think it was just a perfect storm of events that led to his fall.

I'd left him a message that night like I always did before he went to bed, but I wasn't too worried when I didn't hear back. I knew he was with clients on the boat, so I figured he was busy. I sent him one of those meme messages, the kind where a little mouse mimics your facial gestures. I sent it around midnight, and he drowned shortly after that, around 12:30. That night, I had a hard time sleeping, which wasn't unusual for me, but it felt different.

I eventually fell asleep around 3 am, and not long after, my dog started barking. She's small and always barks first, but then our lab, Sadie, started barking in a defensive way, which was unusual. It was around 4 am. I got out of bed and peeked around the corner. Through our glass front door, I saw flashlights. My first thought was that we were being broken into. Then, one of the flashlights caught the reflection of a badge, and I saw it was the police. They knocked on the door, and I told them to hold on while I put on a robe.

When I opened the door, they asked if I was Michelle Bishop. I said yes, and they asked if they could come in. I thought they were going to ask about something related to our neighbors, maybe the kids, because their car was parked by my neighbor's house. I asked if it was about them, and they said no. They asked if we could sit down, and I thought, "Okay, maybe one of our kids got in trouble."

When I asked what was going on, they said something like, "Your husband has been in an accident."

My immediate response was, "What do I need to do? Where is he? Which hospital?"

They replied, "No, he's no longer with us."

I asked what they meant, and they repeated, "He's passed."

It didn't register for a moment, and I kept asking for clarification. Finally, they said, "He's died."

It was all so wrong. There had to be a mistake. Richard was the only person who could pull off surprising me about all things in life. No way was this real; it was unimaginable. He was going to walk through the door.

What they were saying simply didn't register with me. This was a man who lived life to the fullest. Full throttle everyday. *Go big or go home,* he'd say. I was supposed to go first. His presence here on earth was bigger than death to me. This just wasn't right.

Grief

It took years to accept what happened, and only recently have I accepted his death here on earth.

Grief is different for everyone. The officer asked if I wanted them to stay with me for a while, but I declined. I didn't know them, and I was still in a state of disbelief. I walked to the kitchen like my physical self was empty. Just nothing. Close to a walking zombie of sorts.

The next thing I did was call my dad. I woke him up in the middle of the night and explained what had happened. He said he'd be there soon as he lived in Florida, and that I needed to have someone with me.

My youngest child was still living at home, so I called my girlfriend, and she and her husband came over. I also asked my dad to call Richard's ex-wife, his children's mom, because I thought the girls should hear the news from her, not me. To this day, I think that was the right decision. His oldest lived with her husband in Nashville and arrived quickly that day. His youngest came over immediately.

Soon after, people started coming to the house—friends and family. It was overwhelming, and I was still in shock. I couldn't stop crying. I remember going upstairs at one point just to get away from everyone. People were bringing food with the best of intentions, but it was too much. I laid my head on my girlfriend's lap, and she stroked my hair. It was the first quiet moment I had.

When my dad arrived, I met him at the bottom of the stairs, and I collapsed in his arms. I didn't stop crying until after Richard's celebration of life was completed, which we held that weekend. He and I had discussed cremation, as his mother had not been cremated, and I knew how proud Richard was. He wouldn't have wanted anyone to see him any other way but large and in charge. I wanted to make sure that whatever I did was in line with his wishes.

A lot of people attended the celebration, but after that, life moved on for them. For me, everything stopped.

I remember telling people to stop sending food. The meal trains were thoughtful, but I couldn't eat it all. It was just me and my daughter since my dad wasn't living with us yet. I also had so much to do because, as I said earlier, Richard had left without a will. Everything went into probate and I became the executor or personal representative. I had to follow the letter of the law, even though I didn't like some aspects of it. I had to because I wanted to make sure no one could question what was done or the outcome.

While I sorted through a tremendous web of legal issues—multiple LLCs, different accounts, various businesses, and personal titling mistakes, I gutted the house and took it down to the studs. I needed to do it for my own sanity. Every day, I expected Richard to walk through the garage door. I often found myself sitting there anticipating his physical return. That reconstruction was like a metaphorical rebuilding of my life.

Brittany and I lived in my room while they did full construction. We slept on the floor with just a plastic covering for the door for at least eight months. I knocked out the back of the house, so in the middle of winter, there was just a plastic sheet, and it was freezing. But we made it through.

Another Turning Point

Then, right at the end of that year, in December 2020, I got COVID. Just as we were finishing up all the construction, I fell ill. I didn't realize I had

COVID at first. I'm not the type to complain, and I kept telling myself, "I'm fine, I'm fine." I waited too long, and I couldn't sleep because the cold air felt so good to breathe in. The next morning, I told Brittany, "I think I need to get checked for COVID."

She took me to a place where the Health Department was doing tests, and they told me, "If you were my mom or my friend, I'd say you need to go to the hospital." But I thought, "Let's wait until the evening."

It got worse, and I finally agreed to go. However, I didn't meet the criteria for hospital admission at first because my oxygen saturation hadn't dropped low enough. They sent me home, saying that if my oxygen levels dropped further, they'd fast-track me back in. Sure enough, just hours later, my oxygen levels plummeted, and I had to return. I had pneumonia and COVID and ended up in the ICU.

It was during the lockdown, so Brittany couldn't come in with me. I was all alone in the

ICU. I refused to be intubated because I had sold that kind of medical equipment, and I knew that if I were intubated, at that time, it was unlikely I'd come off it. As part of my medical directives, I said, "Do not intubate. You can resuscitate, but do not intubate."

I kept going, even when my oxygen saturation dropped to 42 or 40, which is very dangerous.

Once again, I was alone and facing possible death. This time, by a disease that literally takes the living breath from your physical body. Boy, isn't this a familiar place?

As weird as it sounds, I felt like I was destined to end up in this place. Richard was gone, I was isolated from everyone. Then, because of the medications and isolation, I experienced what I now think was a hallucination.

There was a little alcove in my ICU room meant for a couch. In my medically induced haze, I looked over there and I saw two bookshelves with many books, and a man—not Jesus, not my husband, but someone else. He didn't scare me. It was like I was looking through fog into this dimly lit library. The man was reclining on a leather sofa, throwing a tennis ball between the two bookshelves. It would come back to him every time, over and over. He kept saying, "It's just time. It's just time. It's just time." Then, it went away.

Just Time

I think that experience gave me a new perspective—that our time on Earth is just time. All of a sudden, you're 58, and you wonder where all the time went, from being a baby to now. People always say things like, "The sands of time," or "It'll fly by…," and at the time, you think, "Yeah, right." But then, as you grow older and survive more of life's ups and downs, you see how true it is. It's just time.

I'm not afraid to die, and I'm not afraid of the process of dying. Within my personal faith, I believe in the opportunity to be at the feet of Jesus, to bow down and kiss His feet. I can see it clearly in my mind, and it's never been a scary thing for me.

That experience in the ICU showed me how precious time was. It's not just about how much time you have, it's about what you do with that time. It's how you live your life that makes it precious.

I believe in different levels of time and energy. Our bodies are energy, our souls are energy. When I saw my husband's body, I knew it was him, but I also knew it wasn't him anymore. The soul is so powerful, and the energy we create through our relationships and actions is equally powerful. That moment in the ICU reminded me that time on Earth is just time. There's time here, and there will be time after this Earth. It made me question: What exactly is time?

I don't live my life like every day is my last, even when I had breast cancer.

I never even used the word "cancer" because I didn't want to give it life. I felt that saying the word would give it power, so I rarely tell people I am a breast cancer survivor. I have no family history of it, no BRCA gene, and I just happened to go in for my 50-year mammogram, and they found it. It was shocking because I felt great.

From COVID to cancer, a lot of people go through the same thing. Surviving is a head game. With breast cancer, I went through everything—from not feeling good enough to worrying my husband would leave me, to losing my husband, to worrying about how ugly I would be after treatment. Even with COVID though, I knew I wasn't ready to leave life; I had children.

And then there's the treatment—doctors, medicine, surgery. It was exhausting. They didn't treat my cancer with chemotherapy, but the radiation burned me from the inside out. I could physically see the burns on my skin. It's not something to dismiss, but I don't give it much voice.

I went through treatment for five years. The surgery, radiation—all of that was within the first year, but I continued the medication for four more years. I didn't finish treatment until after Richard passed, so I was still fighting that battle while I was grieving the loss of the man I loved.

God's Plan

Through it all, I lived to survive, fearing that I wouldn't be there for my children to finish what I needed to do. But I always believed that it's God's plan, and when the time comes, it comes. I'm not someone who feels the need to take risks just for the sake of risk. The biggest risk I've taken in life is being transparent, vulnerable, and authentic. That openness to communicate with others, accept feedback—good or bad—is a risk. But I choose to accept it all.

That's why I say, "Choose You First."

Without you, nothing else exists. If I wasn't present at this moment, we wouldn't be having this conversation. Choosing yourself is living, not in a selfish way, but in a way that allows you to live your best life, however that looks.

I'm never going to stop. I will keep on searching and finding new resources, new things to learn, and new ways to share those new resources with others so they don't have to go through some of the same struggles I did.

Some people don't endure—they end their lives feeling hopeless and unloved. They don't experience the beauty that life has to offer every day.

I went on a walk with my dad the other day—four miles. It was beautiful. I could smell every tree, all the different aromas in the air. There were flowers blooming, cars passing by, the smell of fall coming in, trees sappy and fragrant. I live in a place with really fresh air, and I find so much beauty in being able to identify the plants and trees around me—like noticing an orange blossom or a magnolia tree. That keeps me motivated, knowing there's so much more out there to learn.

Wisdom comes from everyone, young and old, from all walks of life. It knows no boundaries, no race, no religion. It comes from within and leads with the heart. And that starts with having a heart for yourself.

A New Phase

As I write this, I'm thinking about the moment I recognized I was entering a whole new phase and season of life.

It happened after COVID. It was a Saturday. I had already isolated myself after Richard's death. People were still reaching out, but when COVID hit, I really isolated.

After recovering from COVID, it took a while to feel safe around people. I wasn't dealing with just a few little coughs—I had been fighting for my life. So, I was very particular about who came in and out of my space, wearing masks and everything. But eventually, we got past all that. So, to that Saturday…

Our weekends had always been filled with people—boating, entertaining, noise, and activity. But that day, it was just me, sitting in the pavilion. Nobody was calling. They were out on their boats, with their families, with their friends, doing things. And I was alone. I thought to myself, "You know, I like this. I like this a lot."

It took a moment, but then I began to grow into it, really grow. I realized I could do whatever I wanted. For the first time in my life, I got to choose. I had never been able to have that kind of choice before. I had always been a wife, a mother, a sister, a daughter, a businesswoman. But at that time, I didn't have a business to run. I was self-empowered to figure out who I really was, and I needed tools for that because I wasn't sure myself. I was asking, "Who am I?" And I started to embrace personal power and positivity.

I had been feeding my brain love and positivity ever since Richard passed, through things like streaming church services. I enjoyed that because I could be in my own space, hear the word or the message, or choose not to hear it if I wanted. I created that for myself. I also started watching *Super Soul Sunday* with Oprah—she has great guests who offer inspiration and positivity. I was reading more about it, too, constantly immersing myself in positivity, not letting Richard's death pull me down. I even thought back to my study skills class from when I was a kid. Because I didn't do well in elementary school, I had to go to summer school to get into seventh grade. They taught us about time management, calendars, and setting goals. It reminded me of learning about business in my twenties—similar concepts, like from Zig Ziglar or Tony Robbins, all those motivational speakers.

I knew the concept of "garbage in, garbage out"—positive in, positive out. Even if I wasn't outwardly expressing it, I knew I was nourishing myself with what I needed. Even though I felt I'd stopped after Richard died, life moved on, time and people moved on. Focusing on my personal growth was the thing that helped me move on.

We go through seasons in life where people come and go. There are chapters within those seasons. Life never stops. Challenges occur, great things happen, bad things happen, difficult things happen. And it's all about what you bring into your mind and your heart. When I allowed myself to be vulnerable, I was at my most authentic, and that was so freeing.

Every day, I get the opportunity to choose how I want to be free in the moment. It's something internal; nobody else has to know. I'm not looking for external validation. I'm experiencing my true, authentic self without judgment. I'm not reckless, but I'm also not going to let fear or the judgments of others hold me back.

For most of my life, I hid in the background, constantly wondering, "What does this person want me to do? What do I need to be for them?" That's how I was raised.

Truth is, I've often described my family as a pack of wolves—you either eat or get eaten. That's not a healthy environment. Predators in the animal kingdom have a role, but humans who act like predators—whether it's politically or in business—are often praised for being savvy or tough. Yet, as I reflect, I know now that there were times in my life when I was probably not trustworthy either. I might have had money or the appearance of professional success, but at what cost?

I had this conversation with my dad as I was moving forward with a new venture. I told him, "I'm not going to sell out. I've sold out my whole life. I want to help people, and I'm going to stay true to that."

Choice, Hope, and Moving Forward

Choice is powerful. Unless they are held truly captive, people always have a choice. I know people get taken advantage of, and I know people make mistakes. I make mistakes, too. I am flawed, and I'm okay with that. I accept that I'm flawed because everyone is. And for the first time in my life, I'm okay with that. For so long, I wasn't.

People often ask me how I've been through so much and still have such a positive outlook on life. I think that's because my superpower is hope.

Hope for you to know that there is hope. I want you to know that giving up isn't the answer.

I want you to take that next step, that next breath, and seek the solutions, inspiration, and support you need. There's so much out there. So many people in the world have a mission to help lift up our world.

All you have to do is look up, get curious, and step into the world. It's not easy, especially if you've been pushed down your whole life. But with the right tools, help and support, you can do anything.

Through my life, I turned to a practice that saved me, kept me sane, protected me, and helped me not only survive but grow through everything and ultimately thrive. I found this solution by instinct. Now, I practice it on purpose.

This practice led me to what I call my Silent Warrior.

The purpose of Part 2 of this book is to walk you through that practice so you too can find your Silent Warrior and take your next big step into your beautiful, incredible life.

Turn the page…I'll see you there.

Part 2: Life Is The Lesson

The Silent Warrior

It's taken me a long, long time to work out how to grow out of my past. I'm not trying to leave it behind nor will I ever try to deny what happened. It's that past that made me who I am today. I'm eternally grateful for the turning points, events, and people who nudged me along and helped me find my way to where I am today.

I've learned a lot from those who have made a lifetime study of personal development. I've also learned a lot from life itself. Having shared a lot of my story with you, the purpose of this part of the book is to share the core lessons I've learned.

Self-Love

Sometimes, when we think of how to fix life, we think in terms of different pillars. Money, relationships, home, family, health…Maybe because we think that if we focus on one thing at a time, it'll be easier to handle life.

I've found though, that splitting up the elements of life, leads to things being disjointed. Can you really fix money if you aren't connected in your relationships? Can you focus on your health if you aren't nurturing your home?

Instead of breaking up all the practical elements of life, I choose instead to look at the whole person: physical and mental health on one side, spirituality on the other side, and the thing that holds it all together, the heart of it all: self-love.

I see all these elements as connected; as parts of a whole that create a sense of groundedness and balance. I believe that when all these elements are in balance, you achieve emotional fulfillment.

It all starts with love for oneself.

When I think about it, this is the image I see: I imagine myself as the center, with arms reaching out. One arm carries physical and mental health; the other arm carries spirituality; self-love is the flowing energy at the core that creates a unified and electric sense of oneness around it all.

It's not like a table with static, grounded legs; it's more like a dynamic, interconnected structure that flows with connected energy, uniting everything.

The idea that you can separate any element has always confused me. Physical and mental health are as interconnected as a flower on a stem. Each part of your life isn't a superficial standalone pillar that needs a few minutes a day to maintain; they're all integral parts of who you are and how you live your life.

Your spirituality, whatever form that might take, forms the root of your ability to love yourself, to love others, and to accept love. Without that self-love, you will never have it in you to sustain your physical and mental wellness.

There are no separate pillars that you need to focus on one at a time. Everything is connected in a unified whole, like one big, beautiful, inspired, heart-shaped unit.

The thing that holds *everything* together in one intricate structure is breath.

Breath is the essence of life. When I'm faced with confusion or overwhelmed by decision-making, I take a deep breath in through my nose, and I tell myself, "Breathe in life and let go of all that doesn't serve me."

It's my way of calming down and finding clarity. When everything seems chaotic and overwhelming, taking that breath helps me put on the brakes and take the next step.

It begins with breath

In really challenging situations, when people are right in front of you, creating noise and chaos, the first step is to breathe. *Breathe in life and let go of anything that doesn't serve you.* That helps calm you down despite the noise and chaos.

Breath is the one thing that you can control completely. No matter what else is going on around you, you can control how you breathe in and how you breathe out.

I remember, during some of the most traumatic moments of my life, trying to control everything and everyone, and coming to the harsh realization that I can't. I also remember realizing that even though I can't control anyone else, I can control my own actions.

In those noisy, chaotic moments, I learned that it didn't serve me to try to match the volume or energy of the people around me. Instead, I learned that when I remained still and quiet, I got to choose.

When others saw that I wasn't reacting at their energy levels, the situation almost always diffused, calmed, and settled. It's practical physics.

At my husband's death, for example, I remained still amidst the chaos. Instead of being in the middle of it, I stepped back and became an observer. Eventually, people noticed I wasn't reacting, I wasn't going to take on their emotions, I wasn't going to add to the noise, and everything quietened down.

It doesn't always happen instantly. Sometimes it takes a while. Sometimes, if the noise doesn't quiet down, I deliberately choose to walk away, not out of anger, but to create space. And when I step back in, I am amazed at how the dynamic changes.

I call this part of me, the part that can go quiet no matter what, that part that can sit in stillness regardless of the chaos, my Silent Warrior.

It's not avoidance, it's about taking that deliberate action. It's not running away, but creating space for stillness.

I breathe, I let go of what doesn't serve me, I remain silent. If I need to, I walk away, then return to bring a new calm to the situation.

This approach isn't just for interactions with people—it's for life itself.

When I was diagnosed with breast cancer, I experienced the same kind of noise. It wasn't one person shouting; it was all of life. All my fears, my worries, my frustration could have broken me down and added to the noise. But I let my Silent Warrior take over, she helped me grow still, breathe, let go of what didn't serve me, and allowed the clarity and healing to commence.

Tragedies happen. Challenges will roll over you. Frustrations will walk in your door without being invited. That's life. How you face them is what determines whether you struggle or thrive. You can either feed the noise with more noise, or you can go quiet. Pause. Breathe. And choose how you grow out of the tragedy, challenge or difficulty.

Let me say this again: It's not just about interactions with others; it's about how you interact with life and all its challenges. It's about dealing with the noise—the noise of life—unleashing your Silent Warrior and thriving.

I struggled with this idea at first, because I always thought of warriors as going into battle with hard and heavy tools. But not the Silent Warrior. The Silent Warrior brings stillness and a quiet centering that is incredibly powerful.

I'm not telling you to meditate for half an hour a day, not even for five minutes, not even one minute. I'm telling you to take a breath, or two or three, and release what doesn't serve you.

It's simple and it's transformative.

I shared this with my dad when he was struggling with hypertension so badly that it landed him in the hospital.

He said, "Where did you get that from?"

And I replied, "I didn't get it from anywhere. I've just always done it."

And it worked. Just taking a full breath into his lungs lowered his blood pressure and increased his oxygen saturation.

It's not magic. There's a physiological response that happens when you take a breath, breathe in life, and release what doesn't serve you. It affects the brain and the heart, and it brings clarity.

Even during my recent breast mammogram, I wasn't stressed when the technician came in. I had been through it before. I was accepting of whatever came. When she said I needed a biopsy, I thought, "Okay, we'll deal with it."

It's not about making bad things go away; it's about being centered in yourself.

After a life of challenge and struggle, there's no need to fear anything. You already know that you will deal with whatever comes your way. *Just take a breath, breathe in life, and let go of what doesn't serve you.*

What happens when you do this is that everything—mental, physical, spiritual—comes together. You're not fragmented. It all becomes one, and that's what gives you grounding.

Trying to separate all the areas of your life and fix them one at a time just makes things difficult for yourself. When you treat each element of life in isolation (health, wealth, relationships, spirit, mindset…) you are like a wobbly table. It's hard to focus on one thing when the whole table keeps trying to fall over.

But if you take a breath, breathe in life, and let go of what doesn't serve you, everything aligns. You have the mental calm and clarity to deal with whatever comes next.

As much as we'd like it, life doesn't let you finish one task at a time. You know this is true. You try to fix one thing and something else will come up to disrupt you. If you are too focused on that one thing, you won't see the disruption come and it will throw you off balance.

When you can treat everything that comes your way with that calm sound of silence, centered and peaceful; *when you take a breath, breathe in life, and release what doesn't serve you,* nothing can disrupt you because all your actions come from a grounded, rooted sense of calm and stability.

You're not abandoning anything; you're just letting go of what doesn't serve you in that moment. When you do that, the thing that seems to distract you most becomes something you can release, and it goes away on its own.

Consider it from a mother's perspective. You're in the grocery store with a whining toddler. "I want, I want, I want." The knee-jerk reaction is to shout at the child to try and shock them into stopping, or to give in so they'll be quiet, but that doesn't help anyone in the long run. Instead, *take a breath—breathe in life, release what doesn't serve you*—and respond with calmness. Even a toddler will recognize that shift. The shift in your mood and your energy. It creates space for a more thoughtful response, not just a reaction.

I had a moment with my youngest child, who was particularly fussy. I would literally take her out of a restaurant and sit in the car with her. We'd sit there together, in calm and quiet, and she'd react differently because she was out of that environment. In my calmness and stillness, she wouldn't get the response she wanted, and eventually, she'd settle. Then, I could ask, "Would you like to go back inside?" And we would. Silence and calm. Stillness. It's contagious.

Please do not misinterpret, I'm not saying that taking a breath, breathing in life, and releasing what doesn't serve you will result in an instantly calm and quiet toddler. That's completely unrealistic. What it does do is empower you in that moment to respond in a different way which will produce a different response for your toddler.

Silence has always been important to me. As a child, I would hide and run to find silence. But as an adult, I've learned to create my own silence, no matter how loud the noise. I've also learned to be comfortable and secure enough in myself to remove myself from a situation, and then come back when my silence is fully grounded.

When people recognize that they cannot force you into a chaotic reaction, everything changes.

To create silence amidst noise, all you need to do is take that breath. You don't have to say anything out loud. This all happens in your head, your heart, and your body. Take a breath, take another breath, and take one more. Breathe in life. Release what doesn't serve you.

If people aren't hearing you, then calmly, remove yourself, even if it's just going to the bathroom. Take a moment. Then come back to revisit the situation. Remain in silence. Then ask, "Are we ready to talk about this?"

The reason this works every time is because when you go silent, you lead with calmness.

When you practice this, you'll notice a profound internal shift. Silence gives you the ability to center yourself and detach from chaos and everything that comes with it. Fear, pain, worry, frustration. When you give yourself deliberate space, you give yourself time to generate the best response.

It doesn't mean you won't feel the noise or the pressure. It means you get to choose how you internalize it.

When you let yourself intentionally breathe, you will find the power to move through any situation with calm, clarity, and creativity.

I've learned that even in the most overwhelming situations where everything feels like it's spinning out of control, the practice of creating internal stillness can bring a sense of balance.

It's a mindset—an understanding that no matter what is happening externally, you can cultivate peace within yourself.

I'm repeating this over and over on purpose. The more you read these words the more you will internalize them. When you *take a breath, breathe in life, and let go of what doesn't serve you,* and give yourself permission to step away and reassess, you will create that balanced, energetic, grounded core from which your greatest and best self can respond.

Again: take a breath, breathe in life, let go of anything that doesn't serve you.

This isn't about ignoring problems; it's about facing them with the full capacity of your centered self.

One of the most transformative aspects of this practice is understanding that I am never standing alone. Life isn't something to tackle in isolation. The essence of life is a series of connections and shared experiences. Whether it's your family, your spirituality, or even the presence of those you've lost, recognize that everything is intertwined.

When you face challenges from a place of quiet, you will get to draw on the strength of those connections.

You are not just one pillar standing alone. You are supported by all of the aspects that make up your being. It's a beautiful realization that brings peace even during life's most difficult moments.

So, with me now...

Take a breath.
Breathe in life.
Release all that doesn't serve you.

And let's go back to the beginning…

At the start of this book I told you that by the end of it, you'll know why nothing that ever happened to you as a child was your fault. Ever. In the next chapter, I explain what I've learned that has led me to believe that, and how it's helped me make sense of so much.

You Did Nothing Wrong

There's a reason each chapter of my story represents roughly seven years of life. It came about as a result of my research into Rudolf Steiner's work on the Seven Year Cycle.

This perspective resonates with me so deeply and has helped me understand so much about our physical, emotional, and spiritual growth, that I decided to share it with you here.

From Oneness to Autonomy (Birth to Age Seven)

According to Steiner, the phase we go through from birth to seven years old represents moving from "oneness with the mother" to "growing autonomy." It represents the phase of life where we are so connected to "our mother" that we can't tell the difference between ourselves and that other person. Then, as we begin to crawl, stand up, and walk, we start to experience a great sense of personal power and freedom, and the "energetic umbilical cord" is tested, stretched, and is eventually meant to be broken.

The trouble starts when we, as young children, don't have that connection. If we are alone or detached from our mothers (or primary caregivers) in those fundamental formative years, our life is profoundly affected, often without realizing it. This isn't necessarily a bad thing—it just is. Being conscious of this process is important.

So, what does it mean?

If a child experiences safety and connection at that young age, they tend to be more adventurous and willing to step into the world with confidence and courage, knowing there's a safe place to return to.

But when a child lacks that sense of safety at home, nowhere feels any safer than the space they're already in. It's a bit like "the devil you know." If the space you're already in is frightening, and you don't know anything else, stepping into the big, bold, outside world becomes challenging, difficult, and confusing because there's no internal sense of safety. A child raised without early bonding and connection always has a sense of needing protection. They have always had to protect themselves so are always on the defensive. From the beginning, they build shields and armor. They don't know it's not normal.

What do I wish I'd known during those years?

When I look back on those early years, I wish I had known that I was loved. That was the biggest thing. I don't think children understand adult language, but they can understand feelings. As a young child, I just wish I had felt safe, loved, and wanted. Those are the three basic things that could have changed so much for me. I'm not saying my parents didn't love me—I know my dad loved me. His parents loved me, his family loved me, my mother's family loved me. But it wasn't stable, consistent love—it was just moments.

Without consistency, it's difficult for a child to feel secure. It's like trying to grow something without proper nourishment. Rain is necessary for growth, but if the ground isn't solid and full of nutrients, nothing will thrive as it should. That's why those early lessons are so important.

Entering the Next Cycle: Ages 8 to 14

As a child moves into the next seven-year cycle, 8 to 14 years old, we enter our teenage years. The cord of connection from the first seven-year cycle is definitely broken. What does the next stage up to age 14 look like?

It speaks of a fight for and commitment to life—emerging power and testing limits. During this period, there are huge energetic shifts and hormonal changes. It's a shift from being a compliant child to an independent thinker.

Between eight and 14, we become more aware of life beyond the family. We start to become rebellious, as hormonal changes kick in. I remember when I had enough strength to hold back my mother's hand and just knew she wasn't going to hit me anymore. I wouldn't allow it. I knew I could stop it. That was a significant turning point. It's triggered by exposure to other children, families, and different experiences outside of the home.

What Do I Wish I Had Known Then?

If I could have chosen a superpower during that stage, I would have wanted invisibility. If I were invisible, I wouldn't be in harm's way. I wouldn't have to hear my mother berate me. And yet, even though I wanted to be invisible, I didn't want to be gone. That's why the rising rate of suicide among young people is so heartbreaking. I had my own darkest moments of awareness, but I also felt that touch from God, reminding me there was light and that I was loved.

If I were having a conversation with that version of myself now, I'd say, "You're never invisible. Others see you. God sees you. I see you."

During those fundamental years, I was in survival mode. I don't think I could have done anything differently. My defense mechanisms, while a form of self-protection, also put a mask on everything—pretending all was fine.

Growing Into Adolescence

The next stage—ages 14 to 21—is marked by wild emotions, raging hormones, and a deep desire for choice and independence.

Once I hit 14, I sought freedom. I rode my bike to escape the chaos. During this phase of life, I lost my virginity and began to understand my sexuality. It was a time of experimentation—a chaotic phase where I truly began to understand the changes in myself.

I grew up faster than most, and as a result, had to learn faster than other kids my age. My dad, who was very transparent about the differences between men and women, helped me understand relationships. He encouraged me to use my beauty to my advantage—not to manipulate for gain, but to understand my worth.

It wasn't easy though. "Understanding my worth" felt like theory.

That lack of connection and safety at an early age led to a sense of floundering growing up, like there was never a strong foundation to stand on; never anything safe to hold onto.

But You've Still Got to Grow Up

An adult with a disconnected childhood is required to develop their personal sense of self, safety, and security as they grow older and wiser.

It takes time. If your childhood was broken and dysfunctional, then know that you don't have to collapse under the weight of it. Does it mean you're starting behind the starting line? Sure. But the more you accept your past as your past, the more you will be able to build on the resilience and fortitude that carried you through those difficult formative years.

When you accept those years as they are, without blame, guilt, shame, or fear, you're saying, "I am who I am today because of how I started out. I'm here. This means I am not a quitter—never have been, never will be. I'm always up for a challenge, regardless of the obstacles, seeing them as opportunities to grow."

You will fail; everyone does. You will flounder; everyone does. But if you were a child with parents who were not present, you did what you could. And now you get to choose.

Lessons for Parents

Understanding the importance of security in those early years is a critical lesson for parents. It's vital to provide support in those fundamental years to allow children to grow as individuals.

These are natural progressions—you're supposed to be attached to your mother. You're meant to be connected through the umbilical cord. From the moment it's cut, it becomes years of slowly building independence from a place of love and safety. All of these experiences stay in the subconscious, influencing how we continue to evolve.

Choosing to Nurture a Little Soul

You hear advice from people about raising children, but so many get wrapped up in their own stories that they lose sight of the needs of the child. They're so self-consumed that, whether consciously or unconsciously, they neglect what it means to nurture a little soul. And it is a choice—you do get to choose. That's my lesson in every aspect of life: one way or another, you get the opportunity to choose. Even not choosing, is a choice you make.

Understanding those three simple needs (safety, love, and being wanted) influenced how I raised my children. I made a conscious choice to be different. I wanted to make sure they felt stable, safe, and loved. Yes, I lost sight of the essentials at times, focusing instead on providing material things, but they didn't care about having name-brand clothes—they just needed clothes.

I see now that I should have slowed down and prioritized simple moments—like taking them to the park. There were times when I thought, "I'll do it another time," until I realized that those simple moments are irreplaceable.

In terms of discipline, routine, and consistency, I was conscious of being calm. I never took my frustrations out on them because I knew how impressionable those early years were.

Breaking Free from Victim Mentality

None of this was easy. When you grow up and out of a difficult childhood, it's tempting to feel stuck and say, "I can't do this now because I had a terrible childhood."

It's easy to be the victim. I am the best victim there is. I could get someone to feel incredibly sad for me. But living in that mentality is giving away your power. You can choose that path, or you can choose to accept your past and move forward powerfully.

It's your choice to take those experiences and use them to enrich your life. If you don't, you're putting on blinders, seeing life in black and white. You survived. You made it. You've grown up and you get to choose what happens next.

The Power of Choice

When you're raised with fear, you put yourself in a box. It's automatic. When all you know is fear, protection, and defensiveness, anything beyond what you can see and understand seems like a dark, dangerous place. So you stay small and closed in.

But when you punch a little hole in that box and see a glimmer of light, you'll be amazed. You might be nervous. You might tell yourself that you prefer solitude. But if you let that light in, it gets brighter, until you finally see how much goodness is out there.

You can choose to stay isolated in the world, or you can poke a hole in the box and accept how powerful you really are.

I'm never giving my power away again. No one should. Giving away your power is like giving away everything—mentally, physically, emotionally.

When you recognize and accept how spectacular you are, how beautiful you are, how magnificent you are as a creation, your box will melt away.

How do you do that?
> *Take a breath.*
> *Breathe in life.*
> *Let go of what doesn't serve you.*

Raising My Own Children

With my own children, I did things differently. I wanted them to be comfortable with themselves, know their worth, and understand their sexuality. I wanted them to feel safe as they moved into adolescence.

My oldest daughter was perfect until age 14 when she hit a rebellious stage. Even though I was divorced, I maintained boundaries and never wavered. My youngest daughter saw her older sister's rebellion and chose a different path—she was headstrong and independent, just like her mother.

I understand now that each of these stages is a stepping stone—they build upon each other, forming who we become. My journey may have been complex, but it shaped who I am today. I wouldn't trade the resilience, the courage, or the understanding I've gained. Through my experiences and my choices, I hope to continue nurturing not only my children but also myself—to be better, to grow, and to recognize the beauty that life has to offer.

Now, are you ready? Are you ready to *Choose You First?*

Choose You First

Here we are, taking the next steps together. There's one thing I must say before we move into this final chapter of the book. In the United States, I realized that you are not required by the state or federal government to have any type of licensing to be a life coach or a professional coach. But, you know, I've been through a lot in my life, and yet I felt it would be hypocritical not to have some kind of expertise in the art of true coaching. I am a certified professional life coach, master certified coach, seeking my international credentialing, and a member of the International Coaching Federation. I'm not a mental therapist, I'm not a psychologist, I'm not a psychiatrist—and quite frankly, there are people who need those professionals.

What I love about the aspect of coaching is that it's about helping a person navigate their own path to a solution. I remember having this conversation with my dad.

He said, "You know, when you were growing up, I'd tell you to do this and that, and you never would. But now, here you are doing this."

And I said, "Well, back then, I wouldn't do it because you told me to."

If I had come to that conclusion on my own—the way a coach helps someone see through the fog to find the right solution—then that would have felt empowering. I've always thought that giving someone the power to discover their own answers was an incredible gift.

But coaching is also a tool. You need to have information, references, and expertise. If you just make things up as you go, then you're not working from anything tested, tried, and researched, which is why it's important to incorporate insights from other experts. Without learning from those who came before me, I'm just a coach who's lived 58 years and had a lot of life experiences.

With that said, my wish for you is that, in the face of the adversity life inevitably presents, you will have resilience. That you realize you are the author of your own life. You make the determination, through the choices you make—good, bad, or neutral—what the outcome of your story is. That's been true throughout my life, and it means I refuse to play the victim card. Now, that doesn't mean I don't take a moment—sometimes even longer—to feel like a victim. But I don't live in that state. I move through it so that I learn the lesson the experience is offering me. That way, I can pivot when I face a similar situation in the future. I'm not saying I'm going to change everything; I say "pivot" because sometimes I do make the same mistake over and over. I am flawed—we all are—and sometimes it takes me a while to get the lesson.

But even the smallest pivot in your thinking can have a dramatic, impactful effect—positive, neutral or negative.

Like you, I am uniquely created, and whatever I gain from my life experience empowers me. I always have a choice.

There have been times—like in situations involving physical abuse—when I didn't understand that choice. People ask me why I stayed in an abusive situation—as a child, as a wife. The reason is that I didn't know any better. I thought it was normal. I thought it was what I deserved until I learned differently. That shift came through different resources, life experiences, and recognizing that this wasn't the end of my story.

Being Comfortable With Discomfort

Recognizing discomfort for what it is and knowing I can change it was a huge lesson. When you come from a difficult background, it's surprising how much discomfort you will endure without even imagining it could be any different.

So, being uncomfortable and recognizing it is a good thing means you're growing. And as you continue to face and deal with these uncomfortable scenarios, they become normalized, and you reach a new and expanded "normal."

Throughout that growth, you will be faced with an abundance of choice. How you choose determines what that new normal will really look like. It's like sliding doors. "Do I go left, right, or straight?" Will my actions lead to a positive negative or neutral outcome?

It would be ignorant of me to say that every pivot will always lead to a positive change—that's ego talking, not real life. What I would say is that you have a choice: you can remain still, or you can take action.

Change will never happen without action—mentally, physically, or spiritually. It won't happen. Now, whether the pivot is big or small, it will still effect change. Sometimes that change is very small, but it has large consequences. You have to accept yourself in those moments, without any preconceived notions. No one can tell you, "This is what's going to happen if you do this." What I'm saying is, wherever you are, you have the power to change it by your own actions and thoughts—because everything begins there.

When you live from your heart, the mind just naturally follows. I've been scripted before—I've followed scripts other people have given me—and it's never good. But taking action, even when scripted, has still led to change—positive, negative, and neutral.

At this point in my life, I'm very fortunate to know that my best self comes from my heart. I'm not a Rhodes Scholar or PhD, but I am wise, joyful, and filled with love. I can help effect change in a positive way for those who want to take that path because I have empathy, experience, and knowledge that I've gathered from resources, books, and people who have made it their single focus to find solutions to life's problems.

I absorb information like a sponge, but I don't let it feed my ego. I know where I want to live— I want to live connected with others.

Let's Talk About Change

As human beings, especially if we've lived through difficult times, we're experts at talking ourselves out of things. Those early morning hours before dawn are difficult. It's when we hear that little voice inside telling us we're not good enough. Well, let's deal with that now.

In my time, I've found that there are six inner challenges we face as we move from where we are to where we want to be. So, let's talk about those.

#1 is self-doubt

What's interesting is that during the daytime we have so many distractions and noise that it's in the quiet moments when these negative thoughts come out. They're loud, so loud that they often don't stop. Self-doubt for me is, "What if I fail again?"

What's different now is that my thinking has pivoted. When I was younger, the fear of failure was my driving force. I was praised when I didn't fail; when I performed at the proper level. Now, when I think, "What if I fail again?"—because I've been shaken to my core and had to recreate myself—the thought that comes to me is: "I don't give a damn. At least I tried."

That's really where I'm at. I know I'm a Southern lady when I need to be, but in my head, that's the reality: "What if I don't even try?" That in itself is more important to me now than the fear of failure.

That's the mindset shift I've undergone. If I don't try, I stay trapped in my box. Who cares what anyone else thinks? I'm the one laying my head down at night; I'm the one looking in the mirror. It took a lot of practice to internalize that—fact is, it felt artificial at first, but so what? You do what it takes.

I use a lot of positive affirmations from different sources, even from watching children play, seeing the joy they find in simple things like a leaf. They don't think, "What if I fail?" They just explore. That's where my strength, joy, and happiness come from as well—from finding wonder in the small things, from living without that paralyzing fear of failure. By treating life as an adventure and not being attached to outcomes. What happens happens. It's all just an event.

So, once you have handled and understood self-doubt, we move on to #2.

#2 Fear of Change

"What if things get worse?" was the biggest fear I had when I was in that abusive situation. But what if things have to get worse before they get better?

The reality is, life sometimes presents itself in a way where things do get worse. But different doesn't always mean worse—it just means different.

When I ask myself, "What if it gets worse?" I have to remind myself that if it doesn't change, that in itself could be worse.

The question becomes, what if it remains the same?

The likelihood of things getting worse and letting yourself be tormented by the worry and fear of that is only going to feed the monster. You have to have enough inner strength to know that staying stagnant isn't good.

Even as you get older, people say, "Keep moving!" Babies learn to crawl, and then they start toddling around. They bump their heads, they get boo-boos—that's what life is about. You get a boo-boo, you put a Band-Aid on it, you stand back up, and you go on. That's what resilience is at all ages. Yes, it could get worse before it gets better, but doing nothing guarantees that it stays worse and never gets better.

#3 Overwhelm.

Life has thrown a lot on my plate, so yes, I've had issues with overwhelm.

In those moments, when I've felt like I couldn't take another single thing, the best thing I do for myself is stay still. I breathe in life, and I blow out what doesn't serve me.

I blow it out!

I don't have to be dramatic about it—I just take breaths in, and I stay still. In that stillness, I find that my plate becomes bigger, my capacity for handling things expands, and things start to come off the plate as others come back on. It allows me to prioritize, which is so important when dealing with overwhelm.

The reality is, there's a lot on everybody's plate. Being overwhelmed is a valid feeling. But if you're stuck in it and not taking action, staying still can help. Stay still, breathe, understand, and let your mind start to prioritize things so you can move through them. You may not get to everything, but guess what? There's always tomorrow. So if you don't get to it, what's the worst that could happen?

It's not like you're in an overwhelming situation where someone is choking and you need to act immediately. In that scenario, there are clear steps—stand up, ask if they're choking, perform the Heimlich maneuver, call emergency services if needed. You take action because that's the priority. Your life, my life, is worth saving. To feel so overwhelmed that you can't breathe, you need to prioritize yourself first—take a breath.

The kids are screaming, the dogs are barking, craziness is going on, and then suddenly the kitchen burner catches fire. At that moment, you're going to forget the screaming kids and barking dogs—you're going to go right to the kitchen and put out the fire. That's your mental priority happening right then.

When everything is coming at you at once, of course, it's overwhelming. But if you stay still, take some breaths, and start to prioritize, it becomes manageable. You might do it mentally, on a piece of paper, on your phone—whatever works best for you. But it will happen, because nobody can get everything done all at once.

Before we go on, I want to mention completion.

One thing that leads to overwhelm is starting something and not finishing it. People start, don't finish, then start something else, and end up with a bunch of almost-finished tasks. More things pile up, and the cycle continues.

Personally, I am very task-oriented because I recognize that when things aren't completed, they rear their ugly heads again. It's like a weed—you pull it, but if you leave the root, it comes back. And you think, "I know I pulled that weed!" You have to get it all out, maybe even spray it with some weed killer, to make sure it doesn't come back.

That's how I think of tasks. I prioritize and complete them because I don't like the feeling of incompleteness. It leaves me feeling unfulfilled and unaccomplished. I would rather fully complete a small task and feel accomplishment in that, than take on too much and choke on it. You don't eat a 16-ounce steak in one bite—you do it one bite at a time.

If you take a large task and dissect it into smaller tasks, you get to feel the joy of accomplishment every time you complete each part. It's fulfilling and does wonders for your self-esteem.

Even the journey of writing this book took a lot of small moments, days, weeks, and months at a time. I didn't start with a finished book—I've done a lot throughout the process. Most importantly, I made its completion a priority. I did whatever it took. I didn't care what else I had going on—I pivoted, I changed, and I got it done.

If you're completion-oriented, you understand the consequences of not finishing something and how it impacts overwhelm. But what if you're working on a project with someone who likes to start things but doesn't care about finishing? How do you handle that?

That's when you lead. You do what has to be done and you take people with you. Unlike me, my dad is very analytical. He takes forever to make a decision, which drives me crazy. There's a place for both approaches, and that's where understanding comes in. You need to understand why someone isn't completing a task and determine what's holding them back.

Everybody has their own vision of completion. Your vision may not align with theirs, so how do you find common ground? It takes compromise from both sides. I want to get there *now*, while someone else wants to take their time. It's like the tortoise and the hare. I'm ready to go, I have no problem making a decision, and I have no problem living with the consequences of that decision—even if it wasn't the right one. Someone else might stand still in the decision-making process because they're more analytical.

Communication is essential to the success of any project, especially when you have different personalities involved—the supporter, the analyzer, the promoter, the leader. Without that communication, you won't make it to the goal line. It's always about the team.

Someone once said that as a lone wolf, you might get to the end faster, but you won't get as far. That's true. If someone's running down the field and misses the goal by an inch, they didn't score. If they had used their teammate in a better position, they would have scored, and everyone would have won. That's my thinking.

#4 Perfectionism
When somebody is waking up at two in the morning, overwhelmed with change and everything else going on in their lives, perfectionism can really trip them up.

Women often have this perfectionist trait because we are more likely to have been raised feeling judged. Too loud, too fat, too thin, too bossy, too aggressive, too naggy, too flamboyant… The list goes on. It's no surprise that perfectionism is a problem when we keep being told we're not good enough.

The reality is that my own bouts with anorexia were fueled by perfectionism. It was the only thing I felt like I could control at that time as a young person. Often, women who lack control will find other negative outlets that give them some positive feedback in their desire for perfectionism.

Perfectionism is challenging for women, especially from a beauty perspective. Unfortunately, men also have this pressure, but it tends to be focused on their financial prowess. Historically, men were the hunters and providers, while women were nurturers. I'm not trying to be reductive or offensive—I've lived and thrived in a man's world for a long time. Most of my businesses have involved men, and I've done well because my father raised me to communicate effectively with the opposite sex. I feel like I often know what drives them. Even in my own business of outside sales, I felt like I had a shelf life. Some young woman fresh out of college would come in, full of enthusiasm, and I'd think, "Oh, great. Here we go."

But here's the crazy thing: perfectionism, I've found, is messy.

People don't realize that. Perfectionism doesn't just happen. A concert pianist doesn't just walk up to the piano and play flawlessly. An artist doesn't create a masterpiece without effort. It takes skill, practice, dedication, commitment, action, and being uncomfortable. You have to face the roaring lion within yourself.

Perfectionism is messy—it's what you allow others to see, and what you see within yourself.

 # 5 Comparison

Comparison can often drive perfectionism. I'd love to know what point in human history caused comparison to become so deeply ingrained. Maybe it goes back to Adam and Eve—when they ate the apple and saw each other, it may have been the beginning of comparison. "You look different than I do."

It's far more complex than that. I haven't read a lot of studies on why comparison occurs, but I see it everywhere, and it's sad. We compare everything—material possessions, achievements, appearances. Men compare themselves to other men, women compare themselves to other women. We all compare ourselves to each other.

Comparison happens in the smallest of decisions. We compare the pros and cons of each choice. Even something as mundane as choosing a dishwasher: you compare different features. It's human nature. The problem is, we think everyone else is succeeding effortlessly, and we wonder why we can't. But that's not true. People navigate through comparison faster than others, which makes it seem effortless, but you don't see what's happening inside. They may be comparing less or have found a way to think about it later, but it's there.

If you can shift your perspective, comparison can be positive. The biggest comparison should be with yourself. Who was I then, and who am I now? That's that comparison that can truly elevate your spirit. Put in the work to create joy and happiness in your life, then compare who you are now to who you were yesterday.

You carry everything with you—both the positive and the negative. People say the negative is always louder, but who made that rule? My husband used to say, "Put one negative thing out there, and no matter how many positive things you add, the negative will always get the attention."

Who says it should be that way? Society does. It's human behavior. It's how we've evolved through history. We compare where we are to where we want to be, and, if we're smart, we go through the change process to create our new reality. So, comparisons aren't always bad.

I would be lying if I said I never compare myself to others. Of course, I do. But I don't see it as competition. I want to be the best version of myself. If I see something in someone else that I think I could learn from, I want to do that. Comparison doesn't have to be a negative thing. If you're thinking about what keeps you up at night, and you see something that could make you better, why not try it? I lay my head down and think, "I'm going to try that tomorrow." What do I have to lose?

 # 6 Your Past Experiences

Negative past experiences can lead to hesitancy. "I tried something, but it didn't work, so why should I try again?" If that's your attitude, you've already written that chapter—you've already signed off on it. If you think it's going to be negative, then you're right, it will be. That's your mindset. Shake it up! If I stayed paralyzed by my past experiences, I wouldn't be here today. Honestly, I wouldn't. I've had to pivot at every turn. Sometimes it might have seemed worse at first, but then things changed.

I've always had the attitude, "Tell me I can't, and watch me." That's for everybody. Tell me I can't—why can't I? Who says I'm not good enough? I reject that.

Do I want to surround myself with people who don't support my success? No! I've made mistakes, and I will make more in the future. If I lived in the past, I'd be repeating those mistakes over and over again. How exhausting is that hamster wheel? Not gonna do it. Take me off.

Now, I can hear what you're saying. Even now, you might be telling yourself, "This isn't going to work for me. You don't get it. My life was different."

Why are you saying that? Why? Do some soul-searching. Something is driving that thought pattern. Why shouldn't you want to create positive change in your life? Everyone's life is different. We're all unique and original. If you close the door on progress just because you think something won't work for you, you'll never move forward.

I look everywhere for inspiration. I have nothing to lose and everything to gain. That doesn't mean I don't weigh the risks and rewards. I'm not suggesting you do anything that could cause harm, but when it comes to enriching your life and living with less mental anguish, you have nothing to lose.

Now you've got me on my soapbox, and I'm going to stay on my soapbox because this is important.

The more you know about what you're likely to face as you progress through change, the more prepared you'll be to face it down. It's almost like being forewarned is being forearmed.

So, let's talk about the consequences of change or inaction.

Sure, as we live life, we miss opportunities, and with that, we can sometimes feel that we're missing out on rewards. But here's the truth: Only you can determine the rewards for yourself.

Life, making mistakes, missing out on what you should have done, shouldn't be just about consequences—it should be about potential. If you're not willing to risk the consequences to take action, you're choosing to live exactly as you are.

If you're in a difficult place - kids, tough marriage, difficult work, strained relationships... It's hard to know what to decide to do.

I don't want to simplify complicated things, but let's look at it from a business perspective.

When a CEO looks at things and makes a decision, they aren't making a decision based on just one factor. They're using all these different factors and inputs from various departments, and they're willing to take action and risk to get that reward. They're willing to face the consequences, even, if it's important enough, to the point where they can even get fired.

Leaders do not let consequences or fears inhibit them from being action-takers, and we are all leaders within our own families and within our own selves.

To lead effectively, we need to look at consequences a little differently.

Consequences are neither good nor bad. They're just neutral events. Do they have emotions and feelings? Absolutely. **But feelings are not consequences.** That's just all in your head.

What do I mean by feelings are not consequences?

Consequences are events—like not having or getting what you want. That's a consequence of the action you took or didn't take.

So what are the feelings? The feelings are the emotions you attach to not having what you want.

You might feel stuck, but you're not. It's just how you *feel*. You might be still in the moment, but you're not stuck, because as soon as you take just one step, you're moving again.

I'm telling you: "I'm stuck, I'm stuck," I just made a slight movement—now I'm not stuck anymore.

It doesn't take a lot of movement, it just takes one action. That's what I'm saying. Consequences are different from feelings.

Feelings are what we've internalized through our upbringing, bullying at school, what others have said to us, and what we've allowed to echo in our brain as self-talk.

What is that self-talk? These are the thoughts in your head that create the *feelings* that make you feel inadequate, unworthy, unacceptable. You're telling yourself these things. That's why I say self-talk is the most powerful tool you have. The brain is powerful enough to make that shift—to create movement.

Think about movement—wind, water, people—it's fluid. It's a beautiful thing if you look at it in motion. Why wouldn't you want to do that?

Are you going to get stuck sometimes? Sure, but not forever. We're born and we die. That's all that's certain. Everything else has consequences, and people attach different emotions to those consequences. Some are challenged by them, some are saddened by them, but the consequence itself - the event - they're all neutral.

When we look at time management, lack of clarity, communication, fear of failure, and even perfectionism, each one of these carries emotions. But the consequences—the events themselves—are neutral. How good, bad, or indifferent they are is determined by the emotions we attach to them, and emotions are something we can control.

There's One Thing That Will Make the Biggest Difference...
We've talked about this already, but I want to make sure it really sinks in. There are a hundred things you can do every day to make life better, different, or easier. But trying to keep all that in your head isn't fun or easy. So, do one thing that, no matter what you're facing, will help you move forward, get perspective, choose how you feel, and progress. I've done it my whole life, and it's always helped. Every time.

Take a breath. Breathe in life. Release what doesn't serve you.

No matter what is going on, no matter how overwhelmed you feel or how much is on your plate. No matter how huge the project is, or how much things hurt. Take one small step; take a breath, breathe in life, release what doesn't serve you, and be still.

If you try to tackle something huge and only focus on the end, you'll never move forward. You'll be frustrated and feel defeated even before you start.

When you need clarity, when there's too much noise, take a breath. When you need to slow things down and get perspective, take a breath.

Whether I need to save a choking person, put out a fire, or help an 84-year-old father, I need that breath.

But, I can still hear you say, "I've tried and tried. And I've tried and tried again. And nothing works."

First, as soon as you hear yourself say those words, take a breath. Then gather the support you need.

Most of the time, when we try to work our way out of difficult places, we try to do it alone. Either because we're scared or confused, or don't think anyone will understand or accept us if they knew how much we were struggling. But we're all scared, confused and struggling sometimes.

Find your community. Find your support.

When all we have is our fear of failure, lack of support, lack of accountability, and lack of community, it's hard to commit to progress.

You have to take things step by step.

There have been times when I didn't have a support system, and during those times, I relied on motivational videos, peer advice, and words of affirmation. We haven't talked much about words of affirmation, but they are really important to me. Reading those affirmations over and over again is crucial for my success.

Another thing that helped me take control of my life was working on my daily plan.

When I was in seventh grade, I had to go to summer school because my grades weren't great.

They taught us how to study. I don't know if those methods really worked for me at the time, but a few things stuck with me. They've come back to me throughout every decade of my life—things like having a plan and writing out a routine.

I literally write down what I'm going to do that day: I'm going to get up at this time, work out, do this or that. As a child, I wrote it all out and read it every day. Even now, the first thing I do when I wake up is go over my plan. I still follow that process.

Words of affirmation, like "I am good enough," "I am kind," "I am loving," "I am worthy"—these are things I still read to myself every day.

Social media doesn't have to be all bad. It can be great for getting words you need to hear.

Over time, the algorithm has picked up on what I'm looking for, and now I get an incredible amount of motivational content through social media from all sorts of sources. **But you can't just consume it; you have to take action. You**

can't just read it and let it sit. You have to do something with it.

With all that said, there's one thing that, if not done well, will undermine everything and prevent you from living the life you want and deserve. It's this: neglecting the self-reflection and personal growth we've been talking about. Not practicing daily.

From the heart, I can say I've been there and done that. I struggle with it. If I could say "I'm there, I've arrived," then I wouldn't need to keep practicing—but growth is a lifestyle.

Every day, I wake up and choose myself. Even when I feel self-doubt, insecurity, or fear, I still remind myself that the journey is exactly that: a journey. There's no end; there's just the beginning and lifelong road.

If you don't take care of yourself every day, then you're not there for the journey—not for yourself, not for others, not for humanity. If you don't commit to yourself, you will be left with a sense of unfulfillment, sadness, emptiness, and loneliness.

The silence that comes from that can be deafening. I've experienced that kind of silence—where I didn't want any noise, any activity, anything at all—and just being in that moment was comforting, but it wasn't living. If I didn't continue to choose myself first every day, there wouldn't be a life worth living.

That's what I believe. We've been put on this earth to enjoy these moments. I believe in a higher power, and I see that power as peaceful but also full of energy, both inward and outward. It's all fluid. I love that fluidity—the idea of purging negativity and feeling nothing but love and energy. That's powerful. I know I'll never achieve it fully, but I want to create as much of it as I can here on earth. I like living in my little bubble, and I think everyone should find a way to live in theirs. It's about self-love. When you start your day by thinking about yourself first, it's about loving the person you are. When you do that, you create space to love others too.

As humans, we've built this culture that says putting yourself first is selfish, but you know now that it's the opposite. If you have that strength within, you can spread so much positivity into the world—and that can change one person, who changes another, and so on.

Sure, there are selfish people who put themselves first to the detriment of others, but those people aren't in my circle. They aren't part of my tribe. Choosing yourself isn't about neglecting others. It's about living fully. If you're not truly living, then no one else around you can benefit from your presence.

I've lost people who had a huge impact on my life, and I have to hold onto the memories of them, even though they're no longer here to grow with me. If we choose ourselves first and honor ourselves, we're also honoring all the people who helped us become who we are.

I've lived my life beating myself up. I know what that's like. When I say, "Choose yourself first," it's because I've changed, and it's made a difference for me. I choose myself, not selfishly, but to honor those who made a difference in my life—those who are here in the present, those who are no longer here, and those who will be there in my future. One day, I'll be gone too, and I want my life to be an example of what's possible.

It comes down to motivation. What motivates you? Are you motivated to do good? To help others? To be kind? If your motivation for putting yourself first is to harm someone else, that's selfish. But if you put yourself first so you can grow and contribute positively, that's life.

It all takes time. It takes patience.
It's funny because looking back on my life, I've exercised a lot of patience with myself, but in the heat of the moment, I've often been impatient. Reflecting back, I think, "Damn, it took you a long time to get here," but in those individual moments, I felt so impatient and frustrated.

When I had my brain injury, it was particularly challenging because I was an A++ personality, and suddenly, I couldn't walk. I had to learn to walk and talk again, to reprogram my thinking. Things weren't coming quickly, and I remember how impatient I was—to the point of self-harm—because I just couldn't express myself well. I've never been physical towards others; it's always been directed inward.

When I was younger, I had this mindset of "Get it done, get it done now!" I still have that drive, but now I've learned to recognize my limitations and the importance of patience.

I'm usually a quick decision-maker, but I've learned that if I slow down and exercise a bit more thought and patience, my progress is smoother and as a result, it's faster. There's value in that patience. Could someone have told me that back then? No, I don't think I would have listened. It's time and wisdom that help with patience, and the world offers you a million ways every day to practice it!

When you're trying to get somewhere and the car in front of you is moving slow as molasses—don't get road rage. My kids have had it, my ex-husband had it, but not me. I'm just like, "Okay."

In Tennessee, we don't use our horns much. You have to be really flagrant for someone to honk. If someone flips me off, I just smile and wave. But there are other things that test my patience more.

Patience is like a muscle; it needs to be stretched. By doing that, you gain more flexibility in your life.

I'm still a work in progress, always learning the value of patience. Some people can't stand crying babies in a restaurant, for example. It doesn't really bother me, even though I don't like loud noise. But if there's a task with multiple steps and it could be done faster by changing the sequence, that tests my patience. Repeating the same action and expecting a different result—that also tests my patience.

I've learned to recognize how my impatience affects me and others. It's a price we both pay. But I'm growing, and I actually like that. It's the art of sitting still—just stopping and being still. Sometimes five minutes feels like too much, but maybe you just need ten seconds. Or thirty minutes. It depends. Breathing is a great first exercise.

So, what's next for you?
We've talked about action and consequence, calm and patience, but where exactly do you want to go next? What's your vision for your life? Taking action without vision will drive you off the road. You need a roadmap. But you need that roadmap to reflect a vision big enough to excite you.

If life has been hard on you, it's easy to set limitations on your visions. But when you take the attitude of "If you can do it, so can I," then things really open up.

For example, I used to think, "If so-and-so can make six figures, I can make six figures." I achieved that. Then someone I knew was making eight figures, and my husband had seven figures. It made me ask, "Why not me?" Why limit myself?

My dad used to ask us all, "What makes you so damn special?" and I used to get stumped. Now, I can answer him. "Just being me is what makes me so damn special."

We all have our unique qualities. People put on blinders—not just in the obvious ways, but in how they see the world. Who says life can't be viewed through rose-colored glasses? Your vision can amplify your career, relationships, health, or personal growth. Let your mind wander like it did as a child.

I'm big on manifesting—putting it out there. If your vision is destructive, that's different, but if it comes from a place of love and kindness, put it out there.

Visions can be specific. For example, my bathroom had a rotten subfloor. It was an unexpected disaster, but I had a vision for it. I exercised patience and took action, and now it's my sanctuary. I love my bathroom.

You'll notice I talk about action a lot.

Dreams and visions are different; the difference is in the action. Dreams are great, but visions require steps to make them a reality. You need to take action to get there.

It's about manifesting for results. I do it all the time—I live in manifestation. It's not something I've sat down and studied, it's something I've just done. Someone says I can't do something? I say, "Watch me." I literally envision it happening.

As a teenager, I remember going to Callaway Gardens in Georgia for a summer vacation, and they were known for their water skiing shows. I'd never skied before. My mom told me I couldn't do it, but I decided I was going to ski. They gave me the instructions, and the first time the boat pulled me up, I fell badly. I was choking on water, and it was terrible. They were ready to bring in the boat, but I said, "No, I'm going again." I imagined myself skiing across the whole lake, and on the second try, I did it—I skied the whole lake without falling.

That's how I've lived my life. I wanted to be a successful salesperson, even in the copier industry, which people said was the lowest of the low. But it wasn't. It was the best training ground for me—for life and for business. It wasn't easy, but I learned so much from it, and I'm grateful.

I remember thinking, "I'm going to do this," and I did it. I've set goals, had visions, and manifested the life I wanted—whether it was the house I wanted to live in or how I wanted to feel emotionally, mentally, and physically.

After surviving COVID, I knew I wanted more for myself. I wanted to live differently—I didn't want to live in pain or loneliness anymore. I wanted more for my children and others. I still manifest that in my head.

I know for a fact that I will be standing up and speaking my message. So, I see it and take action.

That's how I manifest. I don't know if it's the "right" way, but it's how I've always done it. It's exciting. I've touched so many people's lives, even just a little, and if they got even a smidgen of positivity or insight, that makes me really happy. I give without expecting anything in return, and I do it with joy. It's an awesome way to live life.

Through all its ups and downs. No matter what. Life is always going to happen. Lessons will always have to be learned.

In fact, as I write this, I have a biopsy on Monday. I'll know the results in a week. Pathology takes a while.

No matter what the outcome is, it'll be interesting. Life always throws you curves. When you are going through something like a biopsy, in your head, you will wonder, "Is it yes or no? Is it benign or malignant?"

How you handle the curves that life throws at you, how you deal with adversity, and the what ifs, determine the quality of your days and weeks, hours and minutes.

I used to be utterly detached. I was out of my body, almost looking at it clinically. Now, I'm fully present in my body, accepting whatever comes my way. It's a different way of thinking.

You can either sit there and mentally wallow until you have real information, or you can do something else. That's why I'm moving forward. It's been almost nine years since I was first diagnosed with breast cancer, and the way I think now is so different. Nine years isn't a long time in a lifetime, but the change in my mindset is huge. Facing life with courage—from a place of love and joy—is so important, because life will always throw curveballs.

If you're centered in your thinking, truly centered, then whatever happens, it'll be okay. It doesn't matter what it is, because it'll be alright. I'm not coming off my journey. Until I'm dead, I'm on this journey. There's no end, no finish line—except the end of life itself. I love that I get the opportunity to travel this journey, no matter what life has in store for me.

I used to see finish lines everywhere—like when my kids grew up and I became an empty nester. But there are no real finish lines—just tasks completed, steps completed towards the next step. That's how I live now, and it's made everything easier on my mental state.

So, with me now…

>Take a breath.
>Breathe in life.
>Be still. Be silent.
>Release what doesn't serve you.

One More Thing

Dearest,

I want you to know how incredibly proud I am of you for the courage and vulnerability you demonstrated yesterday, today, and always. Life can feel like a race, but you have a remarkable ability to embrace the precious moments and experiences that each day offers.

Remember, everything in life is a choice. While some circumstances may be beyond your control, your response and reaction reflect your true power. You embody this beautifully. Your imperfections only add to your unique perfection, making you even more authentic and relatable.

Navigating through the ever-changing circumstances in your life takes immense courage. The challenges you have faced and will continue to face only highlight your extraordinary ability to respond in your own unique way. Your resilience is like a gazelle gracefully leaping through the hurdles that life presents.

Understand that pain and suffering are temporary experiences. Recognizing this empowers you to remain steadfast in the face of adversity, and that strength is truly admirable. Keep shining your light, and know that you are seen, appreciated, and loved for all that you are.

My hope after reading this book, is that it finds you in a moment of peace, allowing you to reflect on the incredible journey you've endured. I want you to take a breath and recognize the remarkable strength that resides within you.

You have faced countless challenges. Yet, here you are, standing tall, a testament to resilience and courage. The scars you bear are not just reminders of the pain you've experienced, but symbols of your survival, tools that have equipped you to rise above adversity.

It's important to acknowledge your struggles, to honor your grief, and to validate the weight of your experiences. Each hardship has shaped you into the empathetic and compassionate leader you are today. Your ability to triumph over trials makes you a beacon of hope for others who may be lost in the shadows. <u>Your story is one of inspiration</u>; it shows that even in our darkest moments, there is a flicker of light within us waiting to be reignited. You get to be your own author every moment of every day!

Remember to treat yourself with the same kindness and understanding that you offer to others. You deserve love, both from yourself and those around you. Prioritize your well-being and allow yourself the space to heal. It's okay to rest; it's okay to seek support. Know that seeking help is a sign of strength, not weakness.

As you navigate your path forward, embrace your journey with pride. Celebrate your achievements, no matter how small they may seem. Every step you take is a victory, a testament to your unwavering spirit. You are more than your struggles; you are a warrior, a leader, and a source of inspiration.

Continue to nurture your passions and dreams. The world needs your light, your voice, and your strength.

Self-love is not a destination but a continual journey.

Treat yourself gently, encourage your growth, and celebrate your uniqueness.

You are worthy of all the love and joy life has to offer. Never forget the power you hold within yourself. You are enough, just as you are.

Choose You First!

Remember to Live Your Best You,
Michelle

To receive updates from me, schedule a "Listening Session" and join the *Live Your Best YOU* Community, visit:

https://bishoplife.com/

About the Author

Michelle Bishop has faced and conquered numerous challenges in life, making her a true survivor in every sense of the word. From a toxic upbringing and domestic violence to the heart-wrenching loss of her soulmate, battling COVID-19 during the height of the pandemic, and enduring body image struggles, weight loss challenges, and breast cancer, Michelle's journey has been one of resilience and strength.

Her passion lies in helping others move beyond survival and embrace an authentic life of fulfillment. Michelle believes that no matter the hardships, there's always a path to transformation, and she is committed to empowering others to find the confidence to thrive.

As a blogger and master-certified life coach by the International Coaching Federation, Michelle shares her wisdom and experiences to inspire audiences to turn their struggles into strength. In addition, she is a writer, public speaker, life coach, and social media motivator, dedicated to guiding others on their journeys of self-discovery and empowerment.

Thank You

To my forever inspiring grandma,
Your love, wisdom, and spirit continue to light my path. Though you may no longer be with us, your lessons and memories live on in my heart. Thank you for the countless ways you enriched my life and for being a constant source of inspiration. Your spirit lives on in every action I take in my life. This book is a tribute to the incredible legacy you have left in my heart.

To my two incredible daughters,
Your strength, focus, and compassion inspire me every day. You have so much ahead of you, and I have no doubt you will be amazing leaders in your own time. I am so proud and honored to be your mother. Know that my love for you is limitless and will always be with you, guiding you on your journeys. From the moment I dreamed of being your mommy, I knew my heart would belong to

you both. Watching you grow into strong young women fills me with immense pride and joy. I love you more than words can say and am grateful for every moment we share.

To my beloved Richard,
You were my soul mate, the one who opened my heart to the depths of vulnerability and love. In your embrace, I discovered strength in my softness and beauty in my truth. Though you are no longer by my side, your spirit still fills my days with warmth and hope. You were my greatest love, and my unwavering support. Your kindness and affection filled my life with joy and purpose. Though you may be gone, your love continues to guide me and inspire every word write and courage to share the most vulnerable and authentic self. Your actions of kindness to others were always met with strength and dedication. It is our legacy for me to mirror this as I move forward to all that I come in contact within my life. It's the gift that you gave, and I will continue

to give for the rest of my life here on earth as the enduring bond that will forever connect us.

To my greatest love Daddy,
Your unwavering love, guidance, and support have shaped me in countless ways. This book is a testament to the values you've instilled in me and the dreams you've encouraged me to pursue. You gave me life and shaped it with your unwavering sacrifices and boundless love. You have been a powerful source of inspiration and a steadfast leader, always advocating for those who needed it most. Your strength, kindness, and belief in me have guided every step of my journey. This book is a testament to your profound impact on my life and the love you have shown me always throughout the years. Thank you for being my greatest inspiration and for always believing in me.

Always with Love,
M

www.ingramcontent.com/pod-product-compliance
Lightning Source LLC
Chambersburg PA
CBHW071953070526
44583CB00015B/1183